A New Lo

Mercury ƎDAЯ

CH01018693

A New Look at Mercury Retrograde

Robert Wilkinson

SAMUEL WEISER, INC.

York Beach, Maine

First published in 1997 by
Samuel Weiser, Inc.
Box 612
York Beach, ME 03910-0612

Library of Congress Cataloging-in-Publication Data

Wilkinson, Robert.
    A new look at Mercury Retrograde / Robert Wilkinson.
        p.   cm.
    Includes index.
    ISBN 1-57863-013-4 (pbk. : alk. paper)
    1. Astrology.   2. Mercury (Planet)—Miscellanea. I. Title.
BF1724.2.M45W55   1997
133.5′33—dc21   97-14603
                                                     CIP

MV

Typeset in 11/13 Galliard

Cover design by Don J. Moyers

Printed in the United States of America

04   03   02   01   00   99   98   97
10   9   8   7   6   5   4   3   2   1

TABLE OF CONTENTS

Acknowledgments   vii

Introduction: The Magic of Mercury   ix

Chapter 1. What is Mercury Retrograde and
            Why Does it Seem to Cause so Many
            Hassles?   1

Chapter 2. Some Rumors and Observations about
            How Mercury Retrograde Manifests   13

Chapter 3. Mercury Retrograde Psychological
            Patterns   27

Chapter 4. Mercury Retrograde in the Signs
            (Natal, Progressed, Return Charts, or
            by Transit)   41

Chapter 5. Mercury Retrograde in the Houses
            (Natal, Progressed, Return Charts, or
            by Transit)   57

Chapter 6. Mercury Retrograde Periods and How
            They Influence the Different Signs   75

Chapter 7. Famous Mercury Retrograde People   89

Chapter 8. Famous Occurrences During Mercury
            Retrograde 119

Appendix: Mercury Retrograde Positions
            1900–2035 187

Index 195

About the Author 205

ACKNOWLEDGMENTS

I would like to thank three individuals in particular for their assistance in making this work a reality. Coincidentally, all three have Mercury retrograde in their birth charts. First, I would like to thank Betsy. Her Mercury retrograde in Sagittarius has given me enormous insights into the nature of how this phenomenon works, both theoretically and experientially. I would also like to thank my dear friend and colleague Bernadette Ferreira, who has Mercury retrograde in Leo. This work began as a result of a phone conversation with her. What we discussed that day led me to insights around common themes I had perceived with those who also had Mercury retrograde; out of those notes this book was born. And finally, I would like to thank Ferris, who had Mercury retrograde in Aries. As one of the greatest teachers of my life, her non-verbal, whole-vision communication style led me to some of the greatest realizations anyone could ever have about life, love, and the unity of consciousness, Itself.

I would also like to thank the staff at the Reference desk at the Carlsbad Public Library in Carlsbad, California. Their patience, as I researched the significant Mercury retrograde events of the last 150 years, was much appreciated. Libraries are an amazing resource.

Of course this work is dedicated to The Master Hermes Trismegistus; without Him in all his incarnations, none of us would have learned very much about anything at all, and humanity would have made even less progress than it has. Thank you, Master—may this book serve your eternal Holy Work.

—Robert Wilkinson

INTRODUCTION:
THE MAGIC OF MERCURY

When I was younger, I used to marvel at the concept of speed. How fast we could drive, how fast we could talk, how fast we could forget, how fast we could change, how fast everything could end "if the Russians dropped the bomb," how fast you could go from ignorance to understanding, how fast a baby comes, how fast time went by while taking a test; all this fascinated me.

When I got a little older, and started studying such ponderous (and at the time, fanciful!) subjects as Norse, Greek, and Roman mythology, the character that always enchanted me was Hermes, known also as Mercury. Think of it: a god with wings on his feet, traveling great distances with lightning speed, always in the know because he is, after all, the messenger of the gods. Mercury was (and is) constantly in motion, always doing a productive work, charting his own course, well-esteemed and needed by the other gods. In addition, for many years Mercury's head was even on the silver dime!

There were other great ones, of course, who impressed my imagination. There was Thor with his mighty hammer, Odin with his all-seeing eye and wisdom, Zeus with his lightning bolts, Vulcan with his forge and weapons, Ouranos and Chronos with their classic struggle, Hercules the mighty, and Prometheus who dared to defy authority to give infant humanity the divine gift of fire. (That all of these are male gods should be no surprise, as I was, after all, a young male.) With all I learned about the pantheon of the gods, it was still the image of Mercury that intrigued me the most. He was truly a heroic figure in my imagination. He was fast, smart, useful, and well-liked; if there was any way, that was who I wanted to be like when I grew up!

These "gods" and many others (such as the super heroes in comic books) provided my young mind with an escape from the daily grind of living in middle class America with its paranoid fears, harsh competitiveness, technology worship, and arrogant nationalistic self-assuredness. As I grew older, I learned much about subjects more important to America in the 1960s, such as trigonometry, microbiology, oceanography, and marine biology, putting aside my more "frivolous" thoughts about the various gods and heroes. After years of college and many, many courses in psychology, I was introduced (in 1971) to astrology by a friend, quite by happenstance. Though she was an amateur in the true sense of the word, much of what she said intrigued me, and led me to begin to study and investigate astrology on my own.

Initially, one of the things that fascinated me about astrology was that it reintroduced me to my old friend Mercury and his cohorts, many of whom had a planet named after them. And, lo and behold, the planetary attributes were the same as the gods, but to a degree never explored in classical mythology. The adventure of learning astrology began, I was hooked, and remain so to this day.

As it turned out, after having my chart done for the first time, I found that the planet Mercury is not only the most elevated planet in my chart, but it also exactly conjoins my midheaven. Now it all began to make sense. Of course I would want to be like Mercury, if the midheaven describes your ideal sense of honor, profession, and personal flowering!

As I explored the attributes of Mercury and all the planets, the associations multiplied and took on marvelous, magical qualities with every possible new meaning that presented itself. I realized that astrology, and its correlations, gives us a comprehensive interpretive tool to assist our understanding of the larger pattern of space-time. We dance our unique dance of existence within the swirl of an eternal current, whose movement and quality can be known by observing the "vintage" of the moment.

Though we have the energies represented by all the planets active within ourselves, with most people and situations one or two energies predominate. With Mercury so prominent in my chart, it didn't take long for me to realize just how Mercurial I am, constantly exploring, transferring information within and between individuals and groups, both near and at a distance. It also seemed to explain why I have had several professions, sometimes simultaneously. I have been a writer and speaker for many years, and most of the different skills I have learned in a variety of life arenas involve some classic Mercurial function, whether editing manuscripts, hosting a television show, being a corporate troubleshooter, or directing a field hospital for large outdoor festivals. (If the latter analogy doesn't seem to fit with the others, remember the winged caduceus of "the herald"—Mercury—is the classical medical insignia, and that all coordinating functions are ruled by Mercury.)

Mercury, in astrology and therefore in life experience, symbolizes many things. Most of its standard attributes are well known, and can be found in any basic astrological text. For example, Mercury is associated with all forms of communication, analysis, and perceptual understanding. It corresponds to different things in different areas of application, such as its association with the lungs and hands in medical astrology, the media in a national chart, or the electrical system in a car. In a human being, it is identified with the nervous system and the lower, rational mind, as distinct from the higher, abstract mind. Mercury is also associated with the intellect that processes information and all forms of sensory input. It represents the neural system, the sum total of the five senses and the mind taken as a whole principle within us, as well as each of these individually.

All of the planetary astrological glyphs are a combination of three symbols: the circle (Spirit, or pure consciousness), the cross (Matter, or life on Earth), and the semicircle (Soul, or receptivity). There are several excellent books that delve into the meaning of these in depth, which I wholeheartedly recommend for students of symbology; one of the best is *The A to Z Horoscope Maker and Delineator* by Llewellyn George.[1] All

---

[1] Llewellyn George, *The A to Z Horoscope Maker and Delineator* (St. Paul: Llewellyn Publications, 1962).

the inner and outer functions of our reality, symbolized by the planets, are a specific combination of these energies; understanding the symbols will assist you in understanding the various forces at play in all of life.

Mercury's glyph is the semicircle above the circle above the cross; none of the other visible planets involve all three of these factors. Mercury represents the function whereby receptivity to Spirit has been placed above matter, resulting (when perfected) in an elevated Soul-ful personality using Spirit to interpret experience or interact with life on Earth. Mercury at its highest represents Soul using the vehicle of Spirit to express itself in matter. Mercury functions as a mediator, receptivity placing Spirit above all things material. Mercury shows us the way to use pure eternal consciousness as a medium between the Soul's receptivity and the crucifixions of life "fixed" in matter so aptly represented by the cross. Isn't this the true function of our mind? Isn't this where our understanding ultimately leads us?

Our Mercury-symbolized mind is constantly shifting and shape-changing, exploring and wandering within the realm of Divine Mind, also symbolized by Mercury on a still higher level. It is in the nature of the mind to wander, to explore, and yes, to be distracted by ever more information that it seeks to gather instinctively. The mind wanders and roams throughout all the realms on Earth and Heaven, always seeking more information to select, analyze, compare, and compartmentalize. Though it does need some discipline, the mind is here to explore possibilities, not necessarily in a rational, methodical manner. To pathologize the mind's ability to be distracted by new sensory input is to misunderstand its basic function. More on this will follow in the chapter on the psychological attributes of Mercury retrograde.

According to esoteric philosophy, the civilization of ancient Egypt and Arabia began about 40,000 B.C. The founder of that civilization, the greatest teacher of that age, was a great one known as Thoth-Hermes. The Greeks, who came much later, shortened the name of this god-like being to Hermes, and gave him a place in their philosophy and astrology. Still later, the Romans re-named him Mercury. The Egyptians attributed to him the authorship of many ancient Kabbalistic, astrological, mathematical, musical, alchemical, and medical works of antiquity, and as such he is said to have given the world the foundations of modern logic, mathematics, medicine, architecture, astronomy, astrology, and Freemasonry.

The essence of his spiritual teaching, passed down from antiquity, is one of the philosophical underpinnings of astrology. It is best summed up in the ancient phrase, "As above, so below." The planets symbolize basic principles, both within us and outside us. The parallels between the inner and the outer, the higher and the lower, show us how we may know and understand our unique purpose of existence. This cuts across all the fields of experience and all the levels of consciousness. It should not surprise anyone that a being named Mercury (or Hermes) would see life, truth, and consciousness in this way!

Learning to explore anything is a function of Mercury. Exploring all the parallels between the symbols and the substance of our everyday lives is a lifelong task. Even though Mercury is often accused of being a dilettante, flitting from one idea to another and one activity to another, it must have something that persists, as the sheer effort of exploration requires perseverance. Mercury's quality of "persistent oscillation" between the "gods" of our inner and outer life helps us relate different experiences and things to each other and derive personal meaning from them.

In one ancient philosophy, Mercury is represented by the figure of the Magician. It has been said that all magic, and all of the so-called spiritual powers, are simply a knowing of the hidden forces in nature and matter. Mercury just loves to explore all that is hidden! We can infer, therefore, that Mercury can help us know the magical realms of existence. In other lands and mythologies, he has also been known as the Magus, or the Trickster. Any investigation into the hidden realms of existence shows us how our perceptions (Mercury) can play tricks on us, as well as showing us the magic of finding new perspectives, powers, and many unexpected possibilities in our search. No matter what we call this energy, it has an association with the magic in our lives, and the magic in the world.

Karl Kerenyi, the great mythographer and friend of C. G. Jung, called Hermes "The Guide of Souls." He believed Hermes to be a trickster and a thief, the one who brings surprises and changes in circumstances, as well as the uncanny and the mysterious, the supernatural and the superhuman, into any life. Perhaps all of these serve to guide us away from the inertia of the mundane, and into the magical process that unfolds as soon as we understand the function of these in bringing forth our Soul. All that is mysterious and superhuman challenges us to embrace a Soul-ful way of living. This may be the most important function of Mercury in a life.

Mercury is a transmitter, not a source; as such, it has the quality of transparency. Mercury is androgynous, taking on the characteristics of its environment or circumstance. It can destroy as easily as create, and values both equally. Mercury utilizes superconscious energy for the purpose of directing the energies of subconsciousness. In Egyptian mythology, he guided Souls through the underworld. If "the underworld" symbolizes the subconscious, or the hidden side of inner and outer nature, then we can see how Hermes-Mercury represents that watchful directing power in life that guides our outer self (the vehicle of Soul) through the tangled confusions of worldly experience.

Our Mercury-symbolized self-consciousness may act, or not act, according to circumstances. Mercury, therefore, also symbolizes free will, or that power we have to choose how and when to direct our life energies toward creation or destruction. Like the Magician of old, we have the power to manipulate the four elements of matter (earth), feeling (water), mind (air), and Spirit (fire) as we will. If we do not choose to use this divine power to consciously direct our thought-forms, we will be directed by the unconscious thought-forms of our desire nature. Which path we choose determines our character; as we make our character, we make our "destiny." All of this serves to reveal our Soul.

According to Nicholas deVore in his *Encyclopedia of Astrology*,[2] Hermes is the god of science, invention, eloquence, cunning, trickery, theft, and luck in discovering treasure. He is the giver of increase to herds, and the guardian of roads and commerce. In another source, he is said to be the protector of boundaries. Perhaps all of these are involved in finding our genuine Soul function and power on this Earth. It certainly takes Soul knowledge and strength to deal with eloquent and cunning tricksters and thieves, especially when they are involved in the commercial transactions in our lives! Knowing boundaries is very important in knowing our Soul, and regarding luck in finding treasure, if we are guided to our Soul's deeper knowing by inner and outer forms of Mercury, there is no greater luck or treasure to be found anywhere.

In classical mythology, Mercury was never arbitrary; he was defined by his own purposes. He was a unified totality in his own right, with winning and losing equally valued. This is the classic magician: the one who experiments, with all successes simply the result of a correct action taken at the right time, and all failures due to wrong action, wrong timing, or a lack of understanding. A hermetic view sees all life as a grand experiment, with few, if any, moral absolutes. There are no obligations, as everything is a gift from Heaven. All that presents itself in our lives—the kindness and the misfortune—is grist for the mill of experimentation, with all experiments serving to guide and bring forth our Soul.

All that brings forth Soul belongs to the realm of magic, and when we live a Soul-ful life, it is truly magical to behold. There *is* a magical realm of existence, regardless of what our technology-obsessed society believes as a result of too many centuries of Cartesian, atomistic thinking. Mercury, the mythological magus, the trickster, keeps revealing the magical realms of life to us, in ways that delight our hearts and confound our

------

[2] Nicholas deVore, *Encyclopedia of Astrology* (New York: Philosophical Library, 1947).

minds. And we can use Mercury in our charts to show us how we may embrace the magic of our lives, if only we are willing to learn from his most roundabout ways!

Mercury usually moves the fastest of any of the planets, except the Moon (which isn't a planet). Most of the year Mercury moves very quickly, relative to the other functions attributed to the other planets. Doesn't our mind usually outrace every other part of our being? Doesn't magic usually fulfill itself quickly? Occasionally, though, the magical process slows down just enough so we can catch a glimpse of how it works. I believe this is most possible during Mercury retrograde periods.

Each planet experiences the phenomenon of retrogradation at some point in its orbit around the Sun. This is a slowing-down period that will be explained to some degree in chapter 1. Mercury retrograde may be the time when the Divine Magician slows down long enough for us to get a brief glimpse of how his energy works. Perhaps magic can show itself during a Mercury retrograde period, and this is a period when that which is usually invisible becomes visible, and the unknown can become known.

The Magician classically works his or her magic from a place of concealment. In astrology this is hinted at by Mercury's rulership over the mutable 3rd and 6th houses, as these are associated with the signs Mercury rules, Gemini and Virgo. Traditionally all the mutable houses are places of concealment. The mutable houses in the natal chart can give us clues about the Soul challenge to be addressed in the areas of sensation, feeling, thinking, and intuition, and how we may best use the times when these sectors are accented to bring forth the magic of our Soul.

It is hoped that this work on Mercury retrograde will dispel some of the superstitions and illusions connected with this phenomenon. There has to be something productive you can do during these times, and Mercury retrograde periods may be just the times when the magic of life can be explored, known, and demonstrated. There is a magic to life that can be experienced and understood. Maybe the best times for exploring

magical ways of perceiving this reality are these three-week periods three times a year! Enjoy exploring what you are about to
read, take note of past and present experiments and how the
mystery of life has presented itself in your unique journey, and
embrace your magic by being guided to your Soul!

WHAT IS MERCURY RETROGRADE AND WHY DOES IT SEEM TO CAUSE SO MANY HASSLES?

MERCURY RETROGRADE probably has more contradictory interpretations than any other single phenomenon in astrology. It occurs three or four times a year, when the Sun
(actually the Earth) is apparently moving faster than Mercury
for a short period of time. We are not going to discuss the geo-
physics of astronomical motion here. Many good texts already
written explain this phenomenon. In this work we are going to
discuss some of Mercury's possible associations and meanings
within its retrograde context, taking a new look at how we may
best use these energies productively.

   Mercury retrograde is such an easy scapegoat for every
misunderstanding, every misplaced message or unavailable
document. Because Mercury rules many diverse things, it is
convenient to attribute many problems to it. It has "caused"
computer malfunctions, canceled meetings, and delays in everything from childbirth to videotape editing. I have heard
people blame it for some things that have little or no correlation with Mercury at all; regardless of how haphazard the association, still it is faulted for a host of malfunctions.

   With all that it is blamed for, one would think that Mercury retrograde occurs every day. Most people who have heard
of Mercury retrograde believe it has an overriding power to
mess things up, creating confusion in its wake. It is something
many astrologers are mystified by; there is little discussion and

even less agreement as to its possible favorable manifestations. In over twenty-five years of practice, I have heard only a handful of comments about possible Mercury retrograde effects that are not negative. It is universally thought to be the source of general confusion, and conveniently blamed for anything and everything that is going wrong in the moment.

I have searched high and low for books or articles that shed a positive light upon this oft-occurring phenomenon. They are few and far between. For both professional and amateur astrologers, Martin Schulman's *Karmic Astrology Vol. 2* is a pioneering effort in giving all the planetary retrogrades a different look.[1] His interpretations are excellent, offering possible positive and negative behavioral manifestations. It is not a book for the average layperson, however, as it assumes a knowledge of both astrology and psychology, and a belief in past-life influences.

Many people with no background in astrology have heard of this mighty force, Mercury retrograde. It may be one of the best known and discussed astrological periods, but it is regrettable that many people (and quite a few astrologers) are terrified of it to the point of letting their fear rule their activities. Many complain that because Mercury is retrograde, they feel like they can or should do nothing, and can only "wait out the storm." They are frustrated because there are important matters that come up, requiring a decision during the period. A Mercury retrograde definitely does not mean that people should cease functioning!

I have received many calls over the years from people asking me if it is a Mercury retrograde period. When I ask why they want to know, often they tell me they thought there might be a retrograde happening, as some aspect of life is not going as expected, or is confused, or complicated in some unusual way. For example: a friend called to say she knew a retrograde just *had* to be happening because her computer had crashed

---

[1] Martin Schulman, *Retrogrades and Reincarnation*, Karmic Astrology, Vol. 2 (York Beach, ME: Samuel Weiser, 1977).

and she could not get it to do anything. She did not know much about astrology, but she knew that "something *must* be retrograde" because "nothing was working the way it should," that she "couldn't get anyone from the computer store to say when they could come out, or even if they would." She went on to say that she had a deadline she would never be able to meet unless someone, somehow, was able to get her computer functioning again so she could retrieve the needed files.

She was unable even to describe in any great detail what had gone wrong or how. Though I am not a professional computer technician, based on what she was saying I felt that the problem was not very serious. I tried to reassure her that it would most likely turn out okay (I hoped!) and agreed to come over as soon as I was able. When I got there later that day, I showed her some commands that would help her get to where she needed to be inside her computer, and walked her through the steps to help her the next time her computer behaved the way it did. Though this happened during a retrograde Mercury (did you really have any doubt?), it illustrates some of the atmosphere around this mysterious force.

The problem was not serious (Mercury retrograde's much-ado-about-nothing quality). There was a delay in solving the problem (another Mercury retrograde quality). Most of the feelings of helplessness and panic in this situation could have been alleviated by learning a little beforehand about how computers work (Mercury retrograde's after-the-fact quality) so she could have known how to re-boot the system and retrieve her files (Mercury retrograde doing work that needs to be re-done later on quality). The inability of the store to give her a definite time that a service person could come out demonstrates the Mercury retrograde's lack of clear commitment. There was the Mercury retrograde potential to miss a crucial deadline, and of course all this concerned a computer and a journalist, both associated with Mercury!

Though this was a classic Mercury retrograde situation, remember that computer malfunctions occur with great frequency, whether Mercury or any other planet is retrograde or not. Also, certain Mercurial occupations are more likely to suffer computer problems, because computers are part of the job. Not every computer crashes during Mercury retrograde, any more than every relationship crashes during Venus retrograde, or every surgeon's skills crash when Mars is retrograde. Of course, it also seems that many unwanted and unanticipated computer problems present themselves during Mercury retrograde, and that computers, automobiles, lawn mowers, answering machines, tape players, and other electrical-mechanical devices purchased shortly before or during Mercury retrograde malfunction with greater frequency and speed than those purchased at other times!

To illustrate: thinking to "beat the deadline," I bought a state-of-the-art answering machine just prior to a Mercury retrograde period. It proceeded to malfunction three times in five weeks, each time needing repairs. Then there was the tape player that would not work right when I tried to use it, but would work perfectly every time a repairman looked at it! This also happened several times over the years regarding some mysterious sounds my car would make for me, but not for my mechanic. Each of these situations seemed easily attributed to Mercury retrograde. Still, we cannot put our lives on hold when Mercury goes retrograde; phone calls come, tapes need to get made, life goes on. So how do we best deal with the entire notion of retrogrades, making them work for us rather than against us?

BEHIND THE VEIL OF MERCURY RETROGRADE

Throughout the year, usually one or more planets are retrograde. Sometimes there are as many as four to six retrogrades occurring simultaneously. Theoretically you could have as many as eight at once, but that is extremely rare. A planet, when retrograde, simply indicates a slowing of its orbital speed relative to the Sun from the perspective of the Earth. Some planets slow for a few weeks; some for a few months. The Moon and Sun are not considered planets, and do not go retrograde, even though they change their speed, at some times speeding up, at other times slowing down. In our solar system, the motion of the planets and the "lights" (the Sun and Moon) symbolize the ebb and flow of the universal life that we all live within.

This is why it is inappropriate to attribute a problem to a retrograde; though there may be some apparent correlation, a retrograde cannot "cause" anything. This may be the most commonly held misunderstanding about astrology and how it works. Any astrological configuration simply symbolizes a state of time within which life manifests. It is true that many things seem to happen because of an astrological association. However, the cause of all that happens (if and when there is a concrete cause at all) is a prior action, or inaction. All that is, all that occurs, is a part of a larger natural process of unfoldment. All our experiences give us opportunities to be led out of ignorance and fear of the unknown into a greater awareness of the interrelationships between all things.

Though there are many negative things said about it, I feel that Mercury retrograde undeservedly has been given a very bad reputation. It is true that during a Mercury retrograde period, there always seems to be confusion or indecision about what presents itself. Usually people who know about Mercury retrograde hope that whatever the issue, it will resolve itself in some magical way at the correct time if they only wait out the retrograde period. If this reasoning is applied to all retrogrades, you will find that there are only a few days a year when we can expect nothing to go wrong. Obviously this is not the case, as many positive developments do occur during the different planetary retrograde periods.

A Mercury retrograde period does indeed seem to be the cause of many automobile problems, both electrical and mechanical. Are there any other kinds, other than accidents? Mercury retrograde is also blamed for delayed messages, misunderstandings, unforeseen interruptions, and so forth. These kinds of events also occur when Mercury is not retrograde. Perhaps when some part of our car fails during Mercury retrograde, it is telling us we cannot put off needed auto maintenance indefinitely! If we do it well before Mercury begins to slow down, we will not need to do it during Mercury retrograde. Perhaps Mercury here is teaching us to listen to our inner promptings, or that the clunking we hear really does need to be fixed!

When a tape recorder or answering machine go on the fritz, it is often due to sloppy assembly or a faulty part, and the problem inevitably would have showed itself at some point. Maybe it was even manufactured during a previous Mercury retrograde, and now the chickens of faulty assembly are coming home to roost! I once had a tape recorder that had an internal short circuit, but I did not know it until the next Mercury retrograde period, when my new batteries were unexpectedly drained. Mercury retrograde may indicate the time when flaws in certain machines show themselves.

Some of the other widely held superstitions about Mercury retrograde are that it "causes" misunderstandings, interruptions, and delays. When misunderstandings occur, we can learn to be more attentive to what we think we have heard or said, or perhaps think of how we will be understood by another before we speak. All misunderstandings challenge us to examine our word-imagery, so that we do not continue to take our communication style and content for granted. The same word can mean vastly different things to two different people. One constructive use of a Mercury retrograde period is that it can give us glimpses into how another might interpret what we have said from a different point of view.

Similarly, interruptions give us the opportunity to learn patience, focus, and the ability to prioritize and organize our affairs according to their relative importance to us. Perhaps the interruptions that occur during a retrograde period are cautioning us, reminding us that other things must be taken care of before we can safely continue what we are doing. The time that an interruption or misunderstanding occurs is part of the larger process unfolding in the moment; a retrograde seems to point out the need to take an unusual view of the situation, to focus on the inner meaning rather than the outer form.

Allow me to elaborate briefly on this. We often get hung up on forms: what is working, what is not, the goals rather than the process. Everything that happens in our lives is part of a process of self-unfoldment. All processes encompass the forms within them. Around any process lies meaning for us, if we can pierce through the veil of the outer circumstances.

Individual personal fulfillment is found in our quest for meaning, this originating and arising within the mystery of our life experience. The meaning of anything is to be found in the eternal truths that present themselves within our experience. In order to know what is true for us in any given moment, we must see how external forms and circumstances are symbols of who we are, and what we believe in. Meaning is always behind and around form, but we have to search for it. External processes challenge us to watch the magic, to get beyond fear, and to learn a new skill, or patience.

Mercury retrograde periods give us the chance to examine these issues. We have an opportunity to reorganize our perceptions, thoughts, and understanding along lines more appropriate to who we are now. We are constantly changing, and many changes occur without us being aware of them. Most human crises occur when we realize we need to change our perspective from an old point of view to a newer one. Retrogrades may help us here.

Our usual actions, thoughts, and feelings take on their own inertia through repetition. Perhaps the Mercury, Venus, and Mars retrograde periods are times when we can take a new look at what we take for granted in our personality. Perhaps retrogrades show us new approaches to life, and possible new ways to understand how we think, relate, or act. These offer us alternative perspectives of how we want to be, and different ways to behave. Some of these alternatives could make us greater beings, pointing out a greater good that can change our lives forever.

THE METAPHYSICS OF THE PROCESS

All life experiences give us the opportunity to practice a skill or virtue of some sort, or cultivate a strength by transmuting a previously held belief or unexamined weakness or inability. For example, Mercury retrograde is blamed for delays, in the mail, in making connections by telephone, or whatever. Here it is useful to remember that delays also occur outside of the Mercury retrograde period, and while many delays are avoidable, some are unavoidable. We live in a complex of life activities that we do not always control. Through this we learn the parts we are to play in all that is, as well as the limitations of our humanness. It is through our limitations and the inability to control certain outcomes that we are required to search for personal meaning in the midst of circumstances that we often do not create.

We live within a web of life. The web of the stars and planets and their configurations give us clues about our most harmonious action or non-action of the moment. Astrology can serve to give us a deeper and wider understanding of the time, and our most appropriate response to the requirements of that time. Astrology can show us the what, the whereto, the how and the why, as well as the potential outcome of any situation. It can reveal the interrelationships of all that is, on levels both visible and invisible. It is a road map and a weather report of what is, and what is yet to come.

Even if we use astrology, we still live our own lives and make our own choices. Invariably, we are either acting, not acting, or being acted upon. Planetary configurations are relevant to us in our chosen fields of activity, in our life energies, and the varying circumstances that influence us. An astrological configuration cannot make us act appropriately, or solve a problem in and of itself. Many configurations completely pass us by: the "good ones" do not magically bring expected "good," and the "bad ones" do not visit disaster upon us. Any configuration manifests only to the degree we are living life.

An aspect or a retrograde usually does not become important to us, or to our clients and friends, unless it directly influences something in which we are involved. Then the need to know how to act constructively becomes more urgent, usually in direct proportion to the magnitude of the necessity. The need may have already been there for some time in seed form; the retrograde periods offer us a chance to slow down certain parts of our life for closer examination, preparing for a change that inevitably occurs. This is part of a larger cyclic process of unfoldment when the planet speeds up again in forward motion. Life always speeds up again after a time of reflection, contemplation, and transitional change. One of the benefits of Mercury retrograde is that it provides the time for reflection, which can lead to revitalization after a symbolic fallow period.

I have observed that, whether Mercury is retrograde or not, when deep, inner work is going on, our affairs in the outer world slow down for a time. This can be confusing and even distressing if we are conditioned to identify with outer productivity. Still, when it is time for us to do important inner work, the Higher Self repolarizes our energies in some subtle way, whether we want it to or not. We ignore it at our peril, but we can learn to consciously participate in the dance between the subjective and objective parts of our lives, the forms and symbols of our beings.

Periods of reflection, meditation, and contemplation allow us to take a needed break from routine or inertia. Retrogrades are the natural time to do this. When we turn inward, our Soul connection assists our growth by allowing us to focus on that which we would not address if we were preoccupied with mundane affairs. When we are doing needed inner work, life does not go on as usual. Often the slowing down of our work in the world is a signal that we have neglected some important part of our being, and now these other aspects of Soul reality are intruding from within our deepest and highest selves. These must be examined, and this examining process may take a lot of time and energy.

Any slowing of the external events of our life, the frustrating delays that occur from time to time, have a useful purpose if we can take an unusual point of view. The slowing may be the result of a lack of concentration on the outer swirl of events; things do not occur as expected because we were not focusing on them, but rather on something else, another direction. Sometimes a slowdown in some area of life is simply necessary for the transitional process, much like taking our foot off the gas pedal when shifting gears. External speed and power do slow down, but only as a preparation for renewed energy in a time to come. Nowhere in nature is there constant outward productivity, an unending flowering, or bringing forth of fruit. Everything in nature turns inward from time to time, as a preparation for the next period of renewed activity. As I see it, retrogrades perfectly symbolize these periods.

When a planet goes retrograde, the areas of life that it symbolizes need to be reexamined. It is metaphorically an in-breathing or dreaming, a retracing and reexamining of steps already transversed, digesting and assimilating previous experience. This is when we see these areas of our lives from a different perspective, and we can "see" what motivates us in those areas. This is a time when we can examine the effect that our personal subconscious and the Collective Unconscious[2] has upon us.

When the planet goes direct in motion, we can then resume the familiar process of our evolutionary journey. This is the out-breathing, or the time when we act upon that which we have contemplated. These are times to correct whatever we need to, experimenting with and embracing new ways of liv-

---

[2] In this context, the Collective Unconscious is the unreflective mass consciousness within which we live our lives, as well as the racial-cultural experiences within the personal unconscious mind that are activated by certain specific environmental or social experiences.

ing, thinking, and feeling. Direct motion periods give us new experiences to feast upon, new ground to explore; retrogrades assist us in reflecting upon and sorting through what we have initiated during the direct motion periods.

Up to now we have explored ways that life processes are related to other worldly forms and have briefly touched on some alternative ways of seeing retrogrades and other configurations from a positive point of view. We shall explore much more of this in the pages to follow. Still, there is the practical necessity of dealing with a Mercury retrograde situation productively. When a configuration seems to be causing a problem, the real question is, "How should we act?" Abstractions are fine, but when the "real world" intrudes, how can we use Mercury retrograde to our best advantage? For instance, when the boss is steamed because of a misplaced memo, or a needed check is lost in the mail, what do we do if Mercury is retrograde? We must do something. How can we best influence a positive outcome to this crisis?

Here we find ourselves in a dilemma as to how to act, or how to not act and still keep our job. We may explain that Mercury is retrograde, but that still does not solve the need of how to act during the retrograde period. Perhaps Mercury retrograde is a challenge to cultivate foresight, and learn to pay closer attention to details in timing and method. This can help us anticipate, and possibly avert, potential problems that could arise in any situations scheduled to occur during the next retrograde period.

In chapters 4, 5, and 6 we shall explore possible manifestations of retrograde Mercury in specific signs and houses, as well as how it affects each sign. These applications have four levels and three areas of experience, and encompass all that we know as human-ness.

All the astrological energies work on four interrelated levels, in the three fields of human experience. There is the physical-material level, the level of activity involving the physical aspects of our lives. There is the emotional level of feelings, both natural and learned. There is the mental-philosophical level, from which our thinking and ideological attitudes arise and come forth. Finally, there is the spiritual "karmic" level, the level at which our higher consciousness, our living Soul-Spirit, has its own existence and evolutionary plan. This higher spiritual level is also threefold in nature, but we cannot discuss that here, as it is outside of the topic we are currently examining.

Each of these levels manifests in the three areas of human experience—the personal, socio-cultural, and the archetypal fields. Remember that all astrological configurations are acting all the time, whether we are aware of them or not. Some are working on subtle levels, some on more obvious levels. It is in how cyclic configurations affect us personally that we find the answers to their meaning for us as evolving sentient beings. On any level, in any field of activity, at any time of life, different astrological energies show us our most constructive functioning within the web of life.

The quality of doing, feeling, thinking, and realization in the moment is entirely self-determined, regardless of our harmonious or frictional astrological configurations. Yet there are better and worse times for doing things. This is part of what life is all about. Often good timing determines whether a project succeeds or fails. That is the gift that astrology gives to us all, both client and astrologer. So Mercury retrograde, or any other astrological configuration, actually does make a difference. The trick is in knowing the best difference, taking our personal limitations into account. There are positive and productive manifestations of these time periods, and that is what we shall explore here.

SOME RUMORS
AND OBSERVATIONS
ABOUT HOW MERCURY
RETROGRADE
MANIFESTS

THOUGH MERCURY is retrograde only 65 to 70 days a year, its reputation makes it seem to operate most of the time. Most people are somewhat relieved when these periods are over. However, it should be remembered that it continues to operate directly and indirectly well after its exact retrograde period. Though Mercury retrograde periods are the times in which its influence is the most obvious, there are other times when its influence is indirect. For example: direct motion planets in Gemini or Virgo during a Mercury retrograde will demonstrate a retrograde influence, even though they are not retrograde! A retrograde planet in Gemini or Virgo often shows a Mercury retrograde influence because of Mercury's dispositorship[1] of planets in the signs that it rules.

Other possible correspondences involve a Mercury retrograde sub-influence by decan[2] emphasis or through the antiscion

---

[1] The planet that rules the sign another planet is in is called a dispositor. For example, someone with a Sun in Sagittarius has Jupiter as the solar dispositor, as Jupiter rules Sagittarius, whereas a Sun in Scorpio is disposited by Mars, which rules Scorpio. Any planet in Gemini or Virgo has Mercury as its dispositor, as Mercury rules both of these signs.

[2] Decan: There are 10-degree subdivisions considered to be distinguishing secondary influences within each sign. There are two major systems of decan interpretation in current use, one based on the signs, the other on the planets.

point.[3] Another retrograde manifestation is any solar, lunar, or planetary transit[4] over a span where Mercury was once retrograde. This produces a metaphoric echo, and brings the previous retrograde influence to the fore, even though it may be through a planet that is not retrograde. There are other correlations that manifest even though Mercury, itself, may not be retrograde. These influences can come forth as a result of progressions or transits to natal, progressed or transiting positions.

What I have just suggested are only a few illustrations as to how Mercury retrograde works its peculiar wisdom unconfined to its three week periods. Present retrogrades also influence affairs conceived or started in prior retrograde periods, bringing returns which force us to confront that which was left undone from previous times (which may or may not have been Mercury retrograde influenced). Simply put, Mercury retrograde forces us to deal with the loose ends in our lives.

And what of the millions of people with Mercury retrograde in the natal chart[5] or by progression[6] who plan and execute things? The placement is certainly an influence on the way they do things, even though transiting Mercury may not be retrograde at the time they are doing what they are doing. In fact,

---

[3] Antiscion point: A derived "reflex" position of any planet or point equidistant from the Cancer-Capricorn axis. For example, a planet at 14 degrees Cancer has 16 degrees Gemini as its antiscion, each of these being 14 degrees from 0 degrees Cancer.

[4] Transit: The passage of the Sun, Moon, or a planet over any point in the zodiac. The transiting positions can be known by consulting an ephemeris, or table of planetary motions.

[5] Mercury retrograde in the natal chart means you were born when Mercury was retrograde and you feel its influence all your life.

[6] Progressed Mercury retrogrades occur when Mercury goes "Stationary Retrograde" in the weeks after birth. According to the most popular form of measurement, where 1 day after birth equals 1 year after birth, you may count the number of days after you were born to find out if, and at what year, your progressed Mercury will go retrograde. These progressed Mercury retrograde periods last for as many years as the number of days Mercury is retrograde.

it often seems as though these people's affairs move forward during Mercury retrograde periods. For instance, Dr. Jonas Salk, the great medical researcher who had Mercury Stationary Retrograde in Scorpio at birth, announced his breakthrough polio vaccine during a Mercury retrograde in Pisces! It could be that people with Mercury retrograde are actually more accustomed to the slowed pace, and while the rest of us are adapting to the time, they are working and playing in an atmosphere familiar to them.

Perhaps these are a few reasons why sometimes it seems as though we are in an unending Mercury retrograde period. If we are to make the most of this seemingly unending retrograde experience, it is important to open to the fullest possible understanding of what this influence is, seeing it in the most positive light. To do this will mean exploring the natural limitations involved.

THE DOWNSIDE

Mercury retrograde certainly seems to have several common, apparently negative manifestations. The widespread bad vibes, pessimism, defeatism, paralysis of action, and generalized negative thinking are the most obvious downside associations with any Mercury retrograde period. I have observed that something initiated shortly before (or during) this period is frequently more trouble than it is worth, or may not turn out as expected. Often activities involve many distractions that impede progress, or scatter energies to the degree that all effort amounts to "much ado about nothing." It is as though we take two steps forward, one to the side, one back, one to the side, and two steps forward again. There is a lot of retracing ground already covered, or covering ground that seems unrelated to the goal or focus.

Deflections, distractions, delays, overlooking the obvious while focusing on irrelevant minutiae or overarching abstract considerations, and putting the cart before the horse when making plans all seem to be present during Mercury retrograde. There may be an inability to see the forest for the trees, or the trees for the forest. Often things come to naught, or do not work out satisfactorily on first effort, necessitating a re-working of the idea, the plan, or the approach. Perhaps there is another stage of the work to be completed before the project can move ahead, or some part of the work has to be reconsidered before resolution can occur. Assumptions may have to be re-evaluated, or more information gathered in order for the project to be successful.

THE UPSIDE

Mercury retrograde projects often take interesting turns, have reversals that turn out unexpectedly well, or involve ideas, people, or approaches from the past that return to fulfill the present work. These may involve variations of some theme, or an updating of antiquated information or understandings, giving these a new application. One view is that since Mercury represents mind and the Sun represents life as an on-going process, when Mercury slows down (the real meaning of retrogradation) it gives life a chance to catch up to the mind's ideas previously put forth when Mercury was direct, and ahead of the Sun.

Mercury retrograde can be seen as a "liberating ordeal" of adjustment to circumstances. This is a physical-material world adjustment relative to previous ideas. The idea, or plan, or vision was floated out into the material world, explored, and possibilities spun; Mercury retrograde is the adjustment period, where practical exigencies and necessities must be accepted and acted upon. Mind slows down, matter (life) speeds up; ideation slows down, adjustment speeds up. Theory takes a back seat to process.

Mercury retrograde can indicate a period when ideas long held are finally acted upon. In all probability, the idea originally came during a Mercury retrograde, or from a Mercury retrograde person, and has only been reconsidered during Mercury retrograde periods. Perhaps originally it was not the correct time for a thing to occur, and the Mercury retrograde return comes when real-world conditions have caught up to the need for the idea. Many ideas can only take form after certain transitional technological, ideological, or experiential advances have taken place; a retrograde can bring these earlier ideas to the fore at a time when they can be seen in a new light.

Mercury retrograde is an excellent time for reflection, review, and information gathering. These are times when things take curious twists and turns, not always with a clear outcome, and when symbol, meaning, and perception are more important to understanding than "facts." This is when new, more up-to-date information comes to light, or old information can be utilized in innovative ways. This is an excellent time for reorganizing data, playing with possible applications, while leaving options open. These periods are good for reviewing assumptions drawn from old sources and applying them in new ways, or when unusual points of view prove profitable in roundabout ways. Also, useful, but often overlooked, details in objects, people, or processes can be seen in a new light, and may assist the completion or understanding of whatever is being considered. Thus Mercury retrograde is an excellent time for correcting mistakes, and finishing up whatever was left undone at other times.

One upside to Mercury retrograde periods: it is an excellent time for traveling. Over the years, clients have extolled how wonderful their trips were during these periods. It is true that there were occasional delays, and sometimes the itinerary had to be changed, but isn't this true for quite a few trips? Maybe a journey removes us from our usual routine, and we naturally loosen up a bit regarding schedules and expectations because of the highly mobile environment in which we find ourselves.

Going on a journey puts most of us into an adaptation mode to some degree. Of course this depends on individual circumstances, but Mercury-retrograde business trips often seem to be unexpectedly pleasant, or take unplanned directions that work out to everyone's satisfaction. Sometimes what was planned may not have gotten done, but in many retrograde periods whatever did occur was often revealing and fulfilling to all involved. Maybe because life activity is outpacing mind, we all instinctively relax a little. Overall, I have heard very few negative comments about trips taken during a Mercury retrograde, as long as a good book was taken along, and the person was open to meeting interesting people, having unusual experiences, and adapting to circumstances!

One trip I took to Texas during Mercury retrograde was a real classic. The plan was to do several needed tasks over a two week period, all of which had been postponed from other times, or only partially done. I had to ressurect and sell a car, do charts for several old clients who had pre-arranged sessions on previous visits, get a load of decorative stone for a friend's meditation garden, have a spare tire repaired that had gone flat during my previous visit, and clean out a storage room. Of course, since Mercury was retrograde, none of these happened.

Instead, I had a surprise meeting with an old friend who, because of a hidden agenda, became hostile. On the plus side, there was an unplanned visit with another friend from a foreign country who was unexpectedly and briefly in town for business. There were also unplanned trips out of the town I was visiting to places where I re-encountered friends I hadn't seen for years. Money came in through unexpected sources. During one unplanned journey, I received a surprise introduction to a labyrinth which proved to be psychologically revealing and a delight to wander through.

On that same trip to Texas there was the unexpected return of a friend's (now grown) child from a different part of the world, who neither of us had seen in over twenty years. I found that another friend quit his job after ten years with the agency, intending to go back into something he had done twenty years before. I was re-reading part of a book written by another friend, and discovered several pages missing due to a printing error. This certainly seemed to be an archetypal Mercury retrograde trip—not necessarily bad, but making me adapt more than I would have suspected!

MERCURY RETROGRADE ANECDOTES

One client told me (after several days where we kept missing each other just as Mercury was about to go Stationary Direct) about something that had happened to her earlier that day. She had been shopping in a store next to a busy intersection. Someone walked into the store and bellowed, "Who owns the green Volvo that just hit my car?" After no one answered, he yelled it again, and a person paying for something at the counter said "I have a green Volvo, but it's parked right over . . ." stopping when he realized his car was not where he parked it on the street. He ran outside to see it sitting down the block.

His car had slipped its parking gear, rolled backward down a one way street, crossed the major intersection in reverse, hit the car of the man who was so upset, then wheeled itself backward into a new car lot! Nobody got hurt, but the vision of a car rolling backward down a one-way street is a classic Mercury retrograde picture!

Another person had a car accident in a parking lot, where she had been hit in the rear of her sport vehicle. It had jammed her rear door, which she got fixed. During a Mercury retrograde period two years later, in the same parking lot, she hit another car while backing up. It dented the exact same spot on her vehicle that had been hit before, again jamming the rear door shut. Since two years indicates a Mars cycle at work, it seems as though Mercury and Mars got together to make some frustrating music in this person's life! I suppose that if these two stories typify what could happen when Mercury is retrograde, it would pay big dividends to keep track of Mars afflictions and take extra care when driving during these periods.

In another instance, a teacher planned an elaborate art show for her school during a Mercury retrograde period. She had to call all the donors multiple times to get both the pictures and the refreshments delivered. Then, as soon as the exhibit was up, the theme of the show was changed. This made it necessary to take the pieces down to reorganize which ones would be shown, and how they would be displayed. Shortly thereafter, many of the pieces mysteriously fell off the walls, and had to be re-hung yet again.

Another story comes from a woman who went on a trip with a friend. They were going to combine business with pleasure, and rented a house they had stayed in before. They were intending to make a lot of calls, but the phone would not work. No problem, they thought, as the house had four telephones. None of the phones worked, no matter what they did. Here they had returned to an old place, but could not call any friends or clients they had intended to contact. Talk about retrograde!

Some good also occurs during Mercury retrograde. In one instance, a woman lent money to someone with Mercury retrograde in the natal chart. The person was supposed to pay the money back within a few weeks, but time passed, there was no contact, and the person dropped out of sight. She really thought she had lost her money, until one day, during a Mercury retrograde period, the person popped back up unexpectedly and paid her what she was owed.

One way to use Mercury retrograde productively is illustrated in the following story. During a Mercury retrograde period, a woman went to the passport office to renew her passport, but there were over 100 people ahead of her. (Talk about an unexpected Mercury retrograde delay!) She took her number, and then decided to leave the passport office to do some errands that she needed to catch up on in that part of town. After a while, she got the sense that she needed to return. When she arrived back at the passport office, she found there were only three numbers ahead of hers, and she got her passport renewed in short order.

This is a case where having an alternative plan served the need of the retrograde pace of events. Instead of waiting four or five hours in line, she managed to get many errands done that she had been putting off. Her foresight enabled her to think of things she needed to do that were convenient to the location where she would be, and her subconscious gave her hints as to when to return to the passport office for the least waste of time. Truly a good use of retrograde energies!

In one Mercury retrograde period I got a sudden and dramatic flash into an old friend's subconscious. He has Mercury retrograde in the natal chart, and there had always been some contradictory and troublesome aspects of his character I never understood, even though I had known him for years. Then, a particular Mercury retrograde string of minor, apparently unrelated events led me to the flash of insight about the subconscious foundations of his character, as well as the developmental phase of his life when these patterns had probably been set in the form of interactive psychological games.

I have seen Mercury retrograde show itself when parties have turned into unplanned spiritual gatherings, and vice versa. Of course, I have also had malfunctioning or disconnected answering machines preventing me from making connections, and phone tag that lasts for days. I have been to and heard of reunions that did not turn out as planned, have had old bills I thought were resolved unexpectedly pop up unpaid, found mail lost long ago, and had long-lost tapes show up. As an example: during one Mercury retrograde period, the "lost" JFK assassination film that was overlooked for years surfaced and was made public.

I have seen it manifest as confused creature care requiring me to find new people who then have to juggle their schedules to take care of my pets. Unexpected overseas trips are sometimes presented, all expenses paid, while expected overseas trips canceled, for no particular reason. Spiritual pilgrimages have been paid for by someone else. On an inner level, I have observed these periods as a return home to one's inner roots through "glimpses of memory," or as a time when we can complete a "looking back," to achieve closure on whatever we need to end.

This entire book has been influenced by Mercury retrograde, as could be expected. It was inspired by a phone call from an old friend and student who has Mercury retrograde. I sent the manuscript to my publisher during a retrograde and heard back from the publisher during another retrograde, in a very roundabout way. Also, I originally assembled the anecdotes you have just read during a retrograde, just as Mercury was about to go stationary direct. After a three month delay I finally got around to entering them into the book, during a Moon-Mercury conjunction. When I looked to see where this conjunction occurred, imagine my surprise to find that it was within a degree or so of the point where Mercury would hit its next stationary direct point within a few weeks. Perhaps there is something to the study of sensitive points and cycles after all!

THE MYSTERY OF MERCURY RETROGRADE PERIODS

Things are seldom as they seem when presented within a Mercury retrograde context, whether it is a Mercury retrograde period or a Mercury retrograde person. It is a time when unconscious or subconscious motivations (individual or collective) affect what is seen, done, or communicated, or how it is understood. It is an influence of collective ideas from the past that re-emerge in newer, regenerated forms. It is a mental-perceptual process preparing for a synthesized approach after information gathering, assimilating the new contents, and reconsidering the approach, the vision, the idea, or the perception.

During Mercury retrograde periods, the aroused images of the unconscious, collectively influenced and expressing some learned concept or perception, come to the fore. It often appears, in hindsight, as "much ado about nothing," because the old image may not be relevant within a contemporary context. Here the idea, concept, or perception may best be seen as a symbol to be revived in some form relevant to the individual or society at a later date, after life conditions (symbolized by the Sun) have caught up to and surpassed the present uncertainty of perception (Mercury retrograde). After the inferior conjunction, this is presumed to have already happened. Mercury retrograde periods are times when alternative approaches present themselves from the collective mind. These ideas may have their source in the past, or in the future-in-the-becoming. If space and time distinctions exist only in the minds and perceptual mechanisms of three-dimensional lifeforms, then Mercury retrograde may indicate when we are most open to ideas from the distant past—or the distant future. Perhaps we are then more open to different understandings, interpretations, and applications of seed ideas originating in the universal mind.

These periods indicate when unconscious factors of being are aroused, when symbols are made alive to be understood by the conscious, linear, rational mind. The unconscious parts of being can, at this time, be repolarized relative to the conscious ego with its ideas of form and structure. This may even extend to the realm of Spirit, allowing a re-thinking of ideals of service and what constitutes spiritual truth.

A Mercury retrograde period is a time when we may review our understanding and approach to health, given Mercury's rulership of Virgo. Here I refer to health on all levels, physical, emotional, mental, and spiritual. Any new information we receive regarding health is to be welcomed as an opportunity to grow beyond limitations and habits in thinking, feeling, and acting. A Mercury retrograde period is great for re-considering static values and methods as a preparation for acting in new ways.

These are spans of time when the racing mind slows down, allowing the heart-knowing, the direct experience of a thing, person, or activity, to present itself freed from past perceptions and fast judgments. Then our body-wisdom, or our instincts, can supersede the "knowing" of the mind, with its evaluations and constructs and judgments based on comparing, analyzing, and compartmentalizing. It is a time when these compartments of the mind become blurred, and anything can be experienced apart from previous judgments and evaluations. Thus, it could be said that Mercury retrograde temporarily "alienates" you from old opinions, old judgments, old functions, and automatic behaviors from your past that are curiously out of step with the present situation.

Mercury retrograde periods are times when past "karmic" opportunities can be exteriorized in new forms to be concretized after an information gathering period. It represents a second chance to see things, experiences, and people in a different light from the first encounter, and to understand the value of slowing down in certain areas of life, or to see why a situation was originally delayed.

This relates to something I touched on in chapter 1. Any retrograde is a slowing of the planetary motion relative to its average speed. Thus the retrograde process does *not* begin at the stationary points, but instead may be likened to a gradual in-breathing and out-breathing. The motion gradually decreases in speed to a point of maximum slowness, then gradually increases in speed again over time. The stationary points are where its speed is approximately equal to the Earth's, and show threshold points of significance. These points are pauses in the action, so to speak, frozen moments of seeing a forward vision (at the point of stationary retrograde), or taking one last look at a rapidly receding past (at the point of stationary direct).

The process is slow, and slowing, during the entry into the first part of the retrograde process. This is where one learns to adapt to new rhythms, and explores different ways of learning. The vision of what is yet to be has been seen in the span just before the stationary retrograde point. From that threshold, a re-vision of what has been seen or understood is experienced as Mercury continues to slow, and the Sun begins to catch up to Mercury's position. During the entire retrograde period, a different point of view and a new comprehension proceeds to unfold. The point at which Mercury's speed is slowest is actually the maximum retrogradation. From there, it begins to increase in speed until it approximately equals the Earth's motion, which is the point we call stationary direct. Then, after the stationary direct point, a third and final crossing of the retrograde span of experience is traversed. This is where we understand and synthesize what was observed, evaluated, re-thought, and revised.

A long-time astrological student has Mercury retrograde, and observed that the three phases work as follows: the first phase, up to the inferior conjunction, is the end of the old Mercury retrograde cycle. Things get really crazy and chaotic. It is an extreme phase where one is thrown off balance, precipitating a review of some sort. One cannot go forward with plans, and the current momentum of activity stops.

The second phase begins with the inferior conjunction, and lasts until Mercury begins to again pick up speed. This is the beginning of the new Mercury cycle, and one may notice that intuitive impulses and seed ideas start to come into view. One gets a vague sense of what is to come, but no clear picture as yet. By the end of this second phase, things begin to clear, becoming more concrete as one enters the third phase.

The third phase begins while Mercury is still retrograde, but is beginning to pick up speed, and lasts until it turns stationary direct. This is a time for planning and organizing. New activities, new projects, new ways of life are embraced and implemented. This is the time to follow through on what is already accomplished as idea. Here Mercury is speeding up rapidly, giving momentum to the new directions and ideas glimpsed during the second phase, or the projects put on hold during the first phase.

For an astrologer, the stationary points for all the planets can be most valuable in measuring the process of how a client is evolving in several areas of his or her life. Some of the areas of influence for Mercury include the natal and progressed houses it rules, along with the houses in the solar,[7] lunar,[8] and plane-

---

[7] Solar Return: The chart done each year for the moment the Sun transits its exact position in the natal chart. It is supposed to supply an overview for the year to come, and sensitive points in the timing of events.
[8] Lunar Return: A chart done for the moment the Moon transits its natal position each month. It supplies an overview of the month to come.

tary return[9] charts that it rules. Add to these the houses Mercury occupies in the natal, progressed, and solar return charts, the houses where the stationary points fall in the above charts, and the aspects (the angular relationships between any two points) Mercury makes to the various planets in all the houses, whether in the natal chart, progressed chart, the solar or lunar return charts, or to the other transits.

An extensive elaboration on each of these is impossible, as every chart is unique and specific and general rules of this nature cannot take into account all possible variations. Besides, it might stifle your imagination, and a work on Mercury retrograde certainly should not do that! All that said, chapters 4, 5, and 6 can assist you in understanding some possible ways these influences manifest in the natal chart; from there you should be able to imagine possible influences in the progressed and various return charts, or how a certain transit may reveal itself.

In the next chapter we will explore some of the psychological patterns of Mercury retrograde taken from a personal view and in an experiential context. This is done with the aim of helping people with this configuration gain greater understanding and acceptance of a misunderstood part of themselves. I also hope to shine a light on previous misunderstandings between Mercury retrograde people and their therapists and teachers.

---

[9] Planetary Return: A chart done for the moment a planet transits its natal position. These are mainly done for Mercury, Venus, Mars, Jupiter, and Saturn, as Uranus, Neptune, and Pluto seldom (if ever) return to their natal positions during a normal human life span. A planetary return supposedly indicates the primary focus of that energy in the planetary cycle to come, and thus shows a shift in how one applies those energies in one's life.

3

MERCURY RETROGRADE PSYCHOLOGICAL PATTERNS

WHEN DIRECT, Mercury is moved by its own intentions, exploring what it will on its own terms. It is by nature a self-determined force. People with Mercury direct are moving forward. This does not necessarily mean that everyone who has Mercury direct in the chart is a forward thinker. If that were the case, the world would probably work a little better than it does! It is just that when direct, the function Mercury symbolizes is covering new ground and getting new ideas, as determined by the general focus of the life.

This overall life focus arises from our interpretations of sensory and perceptual experiences. These result in attitudes that have their own inertia. Either we are acting, reacting, or being acted upon, and all this works upon our perceptual mechanism to show us who we are.

We are complex beings living an inner and outer reality symbolized by all the planets, signs, and houses. If we consider Mercury retrograde or direct alone it cannot explain why people believe or express what they do. Remember, Mercury is transparent, and communicates what all the other "gods," or powers of consciousness, symbolize in life. Out of this harmony of the various parts of our being, our personalities arise, and with it our personal focus.

When Mercury is direct in a chart, its own self-determined reference transmits whatever it wants, based upon its personal focus. That is why, though occasionally they may race about in many directions, people with Mercury direct concentrate as needed, moving on to new information experiences in order to fulfill an inner motivation.

Mercury retrograde shows itself differently. It is slower, "backward" turned. This does not mean that people with this placement are not intelligent or bright; in my experience, it is quite the contrary. I have found Mercury retrograde people to be inventive, fairly quick in seeing the unusual, and naturally adaptive in their own special way. They have all been very expressive, have great insights into people, and seem to know the most interesting or unusual ways to get from one place to another, whether driving or in conversation. Sometimes they overlook the obvious, get lost in specifics, and show poor judgment, but so have we all.

One manifestation of Mercury retrograde in the ego structure is that the person seems to feel the constant necessity of answering to others, or taking other's points of view into account. A person with Mercury retrograde is in a constant dialogue with the outer world, always responding to outer voices, always reacting to other's mental or verbal agendas. Sometimes there is the urge to respond to unconscious factors, whether understood or not. There is a constant sifting of multiple sources and multiple applications of information, hoping to make sense in a clear, defined, and simple way of all the possibilities presenting themselves to the exploring mind.

To people with Mercury retrograde, many times the words of another seem like so much babble. They may hear the words, but not understand them in the "usual" way, whatever that means. This is why they often are, or seem to be, unable to get what others are saying at the time they are saying it. This point about the timing of understanding and comprehension is important. It is not that people with Mercury retrograde cannot understand—rather, because their Mercury function operates at a different pace than others around them, their understanding takes its own time to occur. This lag in comprehension is often frustrating to both parties, and a plausible reason for the apparent slowness in assimilating information in a usable form.

I had progressed Mercury retrograde during a large part of my childhood. I remember that though I had a very high math aptitude, I never seemed able to comprehend the information in time to do well on the weekly tests. Compounding the frustration and confusion, I would make close to perfect scores on the midterms and finals. This did not make sense to my teachers or my parents, or me, and was the source of many discussions about "not concentrating," "being too distractible," and other personality flaws. Of course, in hindsight, I understand that I was learning through constant reflection, sifting and exploring ways to apply the mathematical principles until I finally comprehended the subject, in my own way and time.

Perhaps Mercury retrograde people have a reputation for being slow students because they lack confidence that they understand anything thoroughly enough. Everyone else is doing it differently and better, or so it seems. There is the feeling that no one understands *how* they do not understand; they are never fast enough, and there is a constant feeling of needing to catch up. This curious form of alienation leads the Mercury retrograde into trying to imitate what works for others. They tend to defer to other's points of view as part of their natural learning process.

One person with Mercury retrograde said that since childhood she has needed to constantly confirm and clarify with others because her way seems to be so different. She has observed that the way she orders things, or prioritizes tasks, is usually different from co-workers. Her conclusion is that self-aware Mercury retrograde people could develop good observation skills to be used in many areas of life.

ARE THEY CHEATING, OR JUST LEARNING IN THEIR OWN WAY?

Mercury retrograde people learn by copying others until the task or information is figured out. They also love to practice before they have to do something "for real." They are often quick to offer help to another, as it provides the opportunity to practice what is being learned with no direct responsibility for the outcome. So one natural teaching/learning method for Mercury retrograde people involves applicable situations. It may be that theoretical, abstract knowledge of principles is not enough to bring forth comprehension. Instead, it may be necessary to demonstrate how the principle applies in practical situations.

One manifestation of Mercury retrograde is an imitative, roundabout learning process. This is an important factor in the educational development of children with Mercury retrograde. They must be encouraged to learn in their own way, at their own pace, within reason. Given that they are in a constant response mode to external stimuli anyway, they are often distractible. This is not Attention Deficit Disorder. This is a normal condition of Mercury retrograde, and needs to be understood and worked with to bring forth its excellent possibilities.

The ability to juggle multiple concepts and multiple mental tasks simultaneously can lead to a very high level of specialized productivity, if practices of integration are also taught. The mind then becomes a crucible for a special kind of genius, whether of the juggler/magician archetype, or the synthesizer/weaver. Both are required if we are to demonstrate our Soul's wisdom. As I see it, bringing forth this ability to know and integrate multiple perspectives is the responsibility of those who would attempt to teach Mercury retrograde people anything.

Under no circumstances should people with Mercury retrograde be rebuked for not understanding something according to the constructs and concepts of another's standards. In extreme cases, especially when scolded as children, the scolding can serve to drive these children beyond the point of understanding or comprehension. The stress to perform serves as a further distraction, and thus the very anomaly of what is desired is created.

When criticism or punishment occurs, it affects Mercury retrograde people's way and pace of learning. It creates endless repetitive conversations and arguments within themselves with themselves. The natural imitative learning style internally repeats the criticism because it is associated with learning. This leads to self-criticism, followed by other-criticism, endlessly repeating itself. This other-referenced self-referencing is so much wheel-spinning, leading the mind to try to convince the fractiling, disorganized thought process that it is going anywhere that can diminish the stress to perform according to the external standards demanded.

The seemingly endless repetition of thoughts in Mercury retrograde people is partially a result of being constantly interrupted, or compelled to answer to others, during the formative years. If Mercury retrograde children are more easily distracted than children with Mercury direct, then we need to explore other approaches so they can best learn what they need to. The usual parent-child communication problems only exacerbate the potential for misunderstanding.

THE ADAPTATION SENSATION

The challenge for parents and teachers of Mercury retrograde children involves adjusting rules and assumptions regarding communication and comprehension. Adults must allow their childrens' unusual insights to come forth, giving these insights as much importance in the learning process as the memorization of ideas being instructed. As long as children learn what is needed, then does it really matter how they learned it, as long as there is no harm done?

Perhaps mentoring is a more appropriate teaching style for these children than instruction, the latter being the norm for most of Western society. Mentoring involves leading children, at their own pace, out of ignorance into understanding through example, friendly advice and counsel, and direct experience. Instruction, on the other hand, involves pouring ideas into their brains, using lectures, directions, and examples. Instruction involves a great deal of memorization learning the "facts and figures," with the requirements of a class set by some external, standardized structure. The word "instruct" comes from the Latin "to pile upon," "to erect," "to inform," "to build," and of course, "to teach." It is my opinion that Mercury retrograde people do not do well with this kind of teaching style.

All minds need some grounded direction. Mercury retrograde minds, however, seem to do better when allowed to explore many possibilities at their own pace. This mindset poses a problem in our educational system. A mentoring method of learning is not useful to a society trying to standardize the information its citizens are aware of. Unfortunately, in our society more value is placed on regimentation than on originality, and collective mediocrity is often valued more than creative individuality.

This is why people with Mercury retrograde seem somehow out of step with society. Their independent thoughts are usually not allowed to proceed at their own pace. They are constantly being interrupted and challenged by other sensory stimuli. Society wants orderliness, and the way Mercury retrograde explores ways, ideas, and linkages does not regiment very well.

The mind's curiosity creates a potential problem. The mind needs a self-determined structure of procedure. It becomes frustrated when it is overloaded by frequent interruptions originating from outside itself. When these interruptions demand some form of verbal, emotional, or physical response, Mercury's energies are turned inward, in confusion. There is frustration as a result of trying to take too much into account, which hinders the ability to act.

When this type of frustration occurs, the inward-turned mind begins to search for concepts and words that can serve as "keys" to unlock the mystery of how to be or what to say to please the demand of the moment. These keys may or may not exist, but an overloaded and confused Mercury retrograde still searches for the correct words or response to alleviate the stress associated with the interruption. If these stressful interruptions occur frequently, the tendency to be distracted by others may become an anticipated subconscious or automatic response pattern. Where this pattern is present it should be understood and transmuted, or the tendency to be distracted by others will frustrate the ability to act with any consistency.

When functioning productively, Mercury retrograde people have important, valuable, and useful insights. A problematic side-effect of their process is the tendency to deflect the direction of a conversation into minutiae, while they overlook larger, more obvious, considerations. They may also see possible applications of ideas in absurdly extreme ways, or improbable situations. Because Mercury retrograde people see odd relationships between ideas and situations, they have interesting and unusual points of view. Sometimes they seem to get completely off the subject of what is being discussed, but if others are patient they eventually get back to the point.

They may also "put the cart before the horse," or leap to a conclusion based on a presumption that may not be relevant, or which may be improbable. Again, this is where having a spirit of whimsical play, a sense of adventure, and lots of patience serves the one trying to carry on a profound discussion (or even a simple conversation) with a Mercury retrograde!

GETTING TO THE GOAL WITHOUT RUNNING IN CIRCLES

For Mercury retrograde people, the quickest route to any goal may not be the most direct. Since they are intent on enjoying the journey of boundless exploration, it might be necessary to do it a different way, honoring their own unique process. I have found that for these people, the most direct route to a goal involves envisioning the goal as precisely, clearly, and generally as possible, excluding all that is extraneous or tangential. From that unconstricted yet well-defined vision, they must then work backward through steps to reach their present position.

The first step toward any goal is to build the thought-form, the ideal of the potential desired outcome. Mercury retrograde people have to do this without excessive attachment to the specifics. Then they must find an attainable middle step between

where they are and where they want to be. It is like going from
Z to A to M, then filling in the rest of the steps as they are understood or needed. First the end, then the beginning, then the
middle, then the rest. If Mercury retrograde people follow this
step-plan, they will not be overwhelmed by the one thousand
and one possibilities that inevitably present themselves in the
process of attaining any goal. I have found that this roundabout
way of envisioning a plan leads Mercury retrograde people to
the quickest understanding of an effective way to accomplish
any task.

When people with Mercury retrograde attempt to approach any goal directly, they usually find themselves deflected
into an innumerable variety of distractions, sidetracking the
process. Again, I feel this is the result of the constant awareness
of differing possibilities of approach, even if most of these are
irrelevant to the actual task of getting to the goal, or getting the
task accomplished. It is appropriate to explore different possibilities of approach; when it is time to act, unnecessary mental
exploration must be set aside to better concentrate on the task
at hand. When the task is substantially on the way to accom-
plishment, new information can be factored in.

Mercury retrograde students have the same high standards
as others who have Mercury direct. They will pursue a subject
or activity to the end because it is their agenda to explore it in
depth, whether or not it fits in with the timetable of the as-
signment. How much time is spent in a search is not as important to them as the experience of an in-depth understanding of
that which is being explored.

In some ways, Mercury retrograde is almost too meticu-
lous, too thorough. I have observed that many with this configuration are excellent researchers. This is fine, as long as time
is no object and the boss is open to the unusual resources uncovered. Perhaps their meticulousness comes from never quite
being sure of their ideas and perceptions, and so more information is sought to assure that the task is being done right.
They may also be subconsciously searching for some outer signal that enough has been done and now it is time to move for-

ward. Until they get the signal, obvious or subtle as it may be, they will keep researching and sifting until the next overriding stimulus comes in.

The communication process usually does not run smoothly for Mercury retrogrades, regardless of how glib or talkative they may be. There is a tendency to overlook the obvious, because these people are looking everywhere except right in front of them. This can lead Mercury retrogrades to focus on minor details and obscure subtleties, using these to anticipate whatever they think is coming next.

Because they lack confidence in their own ideas, sometimes they take things too literally. They focus too closely on the exact form of words being said but do not comprehend the meaning of what is being said. This misdirects the understanding; they try too hard to get the point, which only drives comprehension farther away. Free flowing communication is made more difficult.

People with Mercury retrograde often attempt to take too much into consideration. This can create stumbling blocks through mental clutter, or a lack of perspective as to the relevancy of their ideas. Having too much going on in conversations can result in a hazy focus leading everyone in directions unrelated to what was originally being discussed. Mercury retrogrades' information may be perfectly correct, but not necessarily relevant to what is being discussed, or for accomplishing an immediate task at hand.

This "focus on elsewhere" can lead to many variations in behavior. For example, there may be a continual attempt to solve everyone else's problems while ignoring their own. They may think that they have said or communicated something that they have not. Here the brain bypassed the mouth, leading to the experience of communication without any real communication taking place. Another form of this misplaced focus is in conversations that go everywhere but have no point, no clarity, no resolution. While this may be satisfactory for people with the retrograde, it can be frustrating to others who are trying to make a point, or come to a conclusion. Perhaps the psychological profile for computer programmers is perfect for Mercury retrogrades, as it seems that both love to tinker around the edges, but neither really likes to finish anything, in a permanent sense. There may be a completion of sorts, but Mercury retrogrades love to keep their future options open!

THE PRODUCTIVE SKILLS OF MERCURY RETROGRADE

One very productive arena for Mercury retrograde energies is teaching. Here ideas developed from constant sensory stimuli can be compared with other interpretations, then sifted, evaluated, and communicated from a multiplicity of approaches. The ability to look backward over any subject can serve to bring forth necessary alternative perspectives about whatever is being taught.

Reexamining the past from different perspectives also serves the evolutionary need of the personality, as it helps put different events and experiences in a new light. We do not need to have Mercury retrograde in our natal chart to take advantage of these qualities; we can do this every time Mercury is retrograde, and so constantly gain understanding of our life patterns.

The ability to re-examine a subject is invaluable for research, as it can lead us to see how a thing is evolving. Seeing the whole process of anything provides a well-rounded understanding, whether of external matters or the purpose of one's life. However, this understanding is predicated on working through and letting go of inner uncertainty or the need to believe in false generalized assumptions stemming from sociocultural biases. False information from others can create inner misunderstandings; when directed toward self in negative ways, these cause Mercury retrograde to malfunction.

The computer term, GIGO, means "garbage-in-garbage-out." A researcher will find what is true only by looking at the "facts" of any process from a proper perspective. If you look backward on anything and base your judgments on incorrect or irrelevant information, you will come to a false conclusion. *Mein Kampf* is an excellent example of this.[1]

All information that comes through your five senses and your mind should be questioned, *must* be questioned, for purity, quality, accuracy, relevance. Is it a simple straightforward idea, or is it cluttered, muddied? Is it a high or low concept or thought? Is it kind, good, or useful? Is the information you are getting true? According to what standard of measurement? What cultural value? Under what conditions? Is it nature-created, or human-created? Is the idea obsolete or timely? Is it relevant to you, either temporarily or permanently? How does this concept further or block your sense of purpose? Is this information scattering or concentrating your energy?

My advice to anyone dealing with Mercury retrograde, whether your own, your loved ones, whether in the past, present, or future of your astrological chart: *To thine own self be true.* Examine everything you think you know from several points of view before choosing what is true. See it all as an experimental work of exploration, observing the consistencies and inconsistencies, the similarities and differences, without thinking yourself better or worse for doing a thing the way you do, or understanding it the way you uniquely do.

Recycle ideas with others to better round out everyone's understanding; offer alternative perspectives and different ways to comprehend situations or ideas or issues. Verbalize other options for how things may be viewed, or use different interpretations of certain words or phrases. Find ways to learn and teach through internal dialogue followed by external, open discussion.

This will involve giving everyone time to consider a subject at their own pace, with everyone offering, in their way and time, their comprehension of what is being examined. There may be few conclusions, but there will be lots of discussion and

---

[1] Adolf Hitler, *Mein Kampf*, Ralph Manheim, trans. (Boston: Houghton Mifflin, 1973).

exploration. Mercury retrograde people delight in pointing out useful but overlooked approaches, possible scenarios, and unusual possibilities. When Mercury is retrograde, it certainly frees up the learning process so it can proceed in a variety of ways that may not be logical—but the learning process becomes a grand adventure nonetheless!

In addition to teachers, researchers, and computer programmers, another very favorable way Mercury retrograde people manifest their mental process is through their organizational abilities. One woman with Mercury retrograde has her own business helping other businesses reorganize whatever is needed in order to run more efficiently, more smoothly, or more humanely. She can do the same for individuals who have a house that needs reorganizing, or a life that needs reorganizing! She has a gift of being able to walk into any confused situation and, in a matter of moments, she can size up what needs to be done, and even offers multiple solutions. She then presents these various approaches to her clients, showing how the goal will be reached each way. Her clients get to choose the method and route they need to take to move toward the vision or reorganization she presents to them. Of course, she also continually reorganizes the furniture in her own home, which makes for interesting surprises every time I walk through the door.

Another excellent application of Mercury retrograde skills is illustrated by those who become spokespeople for others, whether an individual or a group. This allows Mercury retrograde's indirectness to speak that which others have already agreed upon. This position makes for good marketing and public relations executives, where there is a need to take others' point of view into account, as well as considering how a particular piece of information would potentially be received. I suspect that this placement is also good for diplomats, when the object is to say something both relevant and inoffensive at the same time. In all of these public functions, the retrograde quality of being able to review what was said after the fact would be invaluable for the unusual insights into how others received what was communicated.

Another possible Mercury retrograde blessing is its non-verbal communication skills. People with this placement are able to take into account all sorts of signals that give them additional information about what is being said, or how a message is being received. Thus these people have a potential gift for reading body language, facial expressions, rapid eye movement, and even how a given environment is structured, revealing attitudes and priorities of the people in that environment. This makes people with this placement excellent human resource people, as they are constantly taking into account how others are sending and receiving information. Knowing how to see from another's point of view provides them with a wider range of communication possibilities. Other possible applications of this skill could manifest as translators, sign language interpreters, or psychologists. Those with Mercury retrograde in the latter field would probably be more comfortable doing dream interpretation, gestalt therapy techniques, psychodrama, art therapy, or even an "ask the psychologist" radio show or newspaper column.

In the final analysis, whether in the inner world of being, or the outer world of doing, Mercury retrograde represents a slowdown of the Mercury principle. This applies to the natal chart, the progressed positions, and to transits. The same is true of all other planetary retrogrades; it indicates a natural slowing of that planetary function, with all that it symbolizes and influences within our charts.

Occasional slowdowns bring us the opportunity to stop taking things for granted. Mercury retrogrades indicate the time to take a new look at many old issues in the parts of our lives influenced by the Mercury placement in our charts. Since all life is influenced by mind, this obviously covers a lot of ground. These times can give us information about our past that symbolizes trends of potential futures, if only we can learn to read its signals from a different point of view. Perhaps revisiting old assumptions and updating our perceptual files is the perfect application for Mercury retrograde energies. The following chapter explains how Mercury retrograde works in the various signs. Though it is written in terms of how the Mercury retrograde sign positions work in natal and progressed charts, there will be other variations to explore, such as the transit position. Feel free to extrapolate possible applications of these principles, based on your own observations and experience.

4

MERCURY RETROGRADE IN THE SIGNS (NATAL, PROGRESSED, RETURN CHARTS, OR BY TRANSIT)

IN THIS CHAPTER I OFFER possible Mercury retrograde expressions in the various signs. In people with this planetary position, or times when Mercury is retrograde in these signs, you may see any or all of these traits manifesting; much depends on other life (planetary) influences. The negative traits will show more strongly at certain times, but these may always be transmuted through psycho-spiritual efforts and techniques.

I have included sections on Mercury being in its own 11th sign, 8th sign, and so forth. This is an ancient technique involving derivative signs and houses. When I say Mercury in Aries is in its own 11th sign, it means that Mercury rules the sign of Gemini, and Aries is the 11th sign from Gemini when you consider the natural zodiac. When I say that Mercury in Aries is in its own 8th sign, it means that Mercury also rules Virgo, and if you start with Virgo, you will find that Aries is the 8th sign away from it. Mercury in Taurus in its own 12th sign means that Taurus is the 12th sign from Gemini. Mercury in Taurus in its own 9th sign means that Taurus is the 9th sign from Virgo. Astrologers use this technique to understand how various sign and house energies relate to each other.

The example personalities may be taken literally, or can be symbolic of what Mercury's energies in that sign might be like. The phrases that begin "Knowledge comes. . . ." are specifically crafted to bring forth the most effective functioning of Mercury energies as they express through that sign.

Mercury Retrograde in Aries

(any or all of these may apply)

Here Mercury's energies slow down to rethink in an impatient mode. Mercury in Aries jumps from action to action, thought to thought, but seldom finishes anything. Here there is a constant distraction by whatever is new, or whatever is emerging in the now; new ideas are more appealing than old ones. Here Mercury glimpses pioneering insights, or insights about new ground broken by someone else. Misunderstandings may occur as a result of haste. There may be an indirect, abrupt communication style, or the unconscious speaks, bypassing the consideration system. There is a need to express everything yesterday, but also hesitancy or an inability to get "the whole thing" out in an organized fashion. In this sign, activities, feelings, experiences, or ideas are never understood quickly enough, or communicated adequately. Seed ideas may be communicated, but in a way that will not be understood until later; here there is an alertness to seed ideas, but these may be so germinal as to not be utilizable. This position may egocentrically repeat what is obvious, or exaggerate, because of subconscious factors. A retrograde Mercury here is able to verbally nail the subconscious or unconscious issue of another.

Mercury in Aries is in its own 11th sign: Here initiative expresses as its own ambition. This position hurries to embrace its own vision or harvest. Many friendships are left incomplete, or blow up through misunderstandings. There is a possibility of initiatives in world service. *Mercury in its own 8th sign* offers initiative as a renewing force; any new initiative gives a death blow to whatever is old, obsolete, or outmoded. This position hastily embraces desires without reflecting on whether they are appropriate. This is an insatiable desire distracted by other desires, and a constant sense that "the grass is always greener" elsewhere. There may be power struggles between parts of the inward-turned mind. *Mercury retrograde in Aries* argues cases internally.

Personalities: The lawyer, game-player, debater, demagogue, pioneer.

Knowledge comes through direct action and review; knowledge also comes from the unusual past feeding the dynamic future.

Mercury Retrograde in Taurus

(any or all of these may apply)

Here Mercury's energies slow down to rethink in a concretization, or stabilization, mode. This position gets distracted by too much sensory stimuli, its personal aesthetic, and wonders if other's ways are more enjoyable than its own. Mental sensuousness may be a problem. There is a constant internal questioning of values, resources, ways of using what one has, or the worth of anything. Here all value and substance are examined to find a greater stability, security, or comfort. There is a need for mental openness. There are sweet and steady, or slow and stubborn, ways of seeing things others do not. This position pays attention to pleasure, comfort, or stability issues first. Mercury here confirms things with the subconscious mind, or with the sensuous centers of consciousness. It either blocks, or knows, subconscious ideas by alertness to throat sensations. Here sweet thoughts are spoken that appeal to other's subconscious, or there is stubborn thinking or resistance to ideas through wrong focus. This position may indicate sensory dullness or insufficiency. Solid ideas are offered to fill in some practical need. Mercury here remembers old ideas of worth, or values that may have been forgotten but which still reside within the subconscious. It is useful to take a new look at what preserves and endures, or to remember the value of an old experience.

Mercury in Taurus is in its own 12th sign: Here values, worth, or comfort of mental standards are their own harvest. Mercury here is possessive, and may self-destruct by refusing the new, staying stuck in old value systems. This position needs to reflect and sift all past experience to round the understanding. There may be the sensation of drowning in one's own sensory stimuli swamp, which paralyzes the closure function. *Mercury in its own 9th sign* makes value its own truth. *Mercury retrograde in Taurus* examines substance, facts, values, and resources constantly to see if they are furthering a desired future, or truth.

Personalities: The aesthete, critic, gourmet, artist, financial planner, professor of economics.

Knowledge comes from confirming value; knowledge also comes from expressing gentle constancy for the enjoyment of all.

Mercury Retrograde in Gemini

(any or all of these may apply)

Here Mercury's energies slow down to rethink in an exploration mode. There is either indecision, or thorough examination. Everything is considered, but no firm conclusions are drawn. There is an openness to the "other side of the coin," to other possibilities, and seeing different interpretations of information. Mercury here plays with ideas, as though swinging from one vine to another with no particular direction in mind. This is the infinite maze of the mind's own self-generated dilemmas overly distracted by endless minutiae, resulting in a thousand puzzles to be solved. This position is inquisitive in unusual directions, leading to completely impersonal points of view, and sees unconscious factors as tools to be explored. There may be subconscious blocks to the ability to make firm judgments, or moral-ethical considerations sometimes show as arguments for their own sake. Restlessness can lead to unusual discoveries to be shared. Here paradoxes are resolved through oscillation between points of view, revealing factors not previously considered. There may also be witty verbal manipulations going nowhere. This position fills in gaps in arguments or dilemmas long held, and reframes old questions by asking new questions.

Mercury in Gemini is in its own 1st sign: Here knowledge reveals itself to itself. There is a seeking within for that which is simultaneously beyond and within. All concepts are applied to self, self's experience, and self's prior information first, i.e., "Is this a different take on a previous idea?" *Mercury in its own 10th sign* indicates that the culmination of thinking is knowledge for its own sake. This is the fulfillment of the mind, making distinctions between all sorts of differences, to demonstrate its own authority. *Mercury retrograde in Gemini* claims its right not to decide, or conclude, unless *it* chooses to do so, and then reserves the right to change its mind when it sees fit.

Personalities: The true dilettante, computer programmer, crossword puzzle expert, librarian, debater, speechwriter.

Knowledge comes from exploring impersonally; knowledge also comes from facing the decision, and taking the leap.

Mercury Retrograde in Cancer

(any or all of these may apply)

Here Mercury's energies slow down to rethink in a sensitive, receptive, adaptive mode. The inward turned feeling-dominated mind tests all ideas and evaluates them to see if they bring greater or lesser feelings of security. There is a solving of puzzles and all that can be picked apart. This position uses feelings to communicate as well as using ideas about unsuspected needs. There is a caring communication style able to touch others deeply, and a sensitivity to what others are feeling, even if it cannot be expressed. This position understands other's survival issues. There may be suspicious questioning based in subconscious emotional factors, or uncertainty in self-expression due to old emotional hurts or fears. This position often finds a loving and kind way to look at things due to instinctively knowing unsuspected feeling-factors. Here there is an ability to express a sympathetic view because of seeing situations as another would, or seeing into another's subconscious. This position tenaciously remembers old personal business, and has the ability to mimic others as they are, or may mimic others to fill subconscious or unconscious needs or lacks. Everything may be related to childhood, in self or in others. This position indicates an instinctive mental sympathy with others, with the ability to absorb unusual ideas in order to anticipate needs for future times and situations.

Mercury in its own 2nd sign: Here feeling values itself as a way of confirming what it can draw on, especially to fulfill an immediate need. This position seeks mental substance to further a sense of definiteness, and examines matter's source. It knows the immediate need and communicates that knowledge indirectly, or in terms of another's feeling-based point of view. *Mercury in its own 11th sign* indicates that the goal of all ideas is to fill some need. *Mercury retrograde in Cancer* gives the desire to provide nourishment within a group situation.

Personalities: The locksmith, commodities broker, oral historian, feng shui expert, family counselor, chef, pitchman.

Knowledge comes from need fulfillment; knowledge also comes from offering what you preserve from the past in a caring and sympathetic way.

Mercury Retrograde in Leo

(any or all of these may apply)

Here Mercury's energies slow down to rethink in an expressive, dramatic, playful mode. This is the pride of the mind's own variety and multiplicity; it plays with its own insights, as though swinging from the limbs of a tree. This position measures the applause for, or rejection of, its clever insights. There may be resistance to mental change stemming from pride or power issues. There are insights into how children explore, examine, and process information. This position communicates the truth, nobility, or authenticity in any art form. There may be perceptual laziness or sterile arguments; this is the big talker, needing to see how others are impressed. It is also the position of the heartfelt mind expressing the dignity of an abundant view and noble subconscious. Here ideas are expressed, awakening another's heart. There may be noble eternal thoughts that hold a timeless vision of honor and a regal ideal. This one is able to perceive the grandeur within self, or others, in unusual ways. There may be stubborn, proud, or inflexible thinking based in subconscious fears. Unusual views of courage may be expressed, or love found in unusual perspectives. There may be radiant speaking, communicating a generous point of view, or grand thinking that penetrates other's subconscious.

Mercury in Leo is in its own 3rd sign: This is the mind's pride in its own form of expression. Here joy, play, and spontaneous expression are the perceptual mechanisms of the mind. This is a position where the light of mind shines into many corners yet to be explored, where the play of power will be harvested. This is where the noble and pure aspect of the mind flexes its muscle. *Mercury in its own 12th sign* indicates that pride of mind is self-destructive. *Mercury retrograde in Leo* offers love as the motivator of all communications, and playfulness as the endgame of all ideas and reflections.

Personalities: The sports writer, diarist, race car driver, sculptor, producer-director, cartoonist, school teacher, child psychologist, performer, mentor of the young.

Knowledge comes from enthusiasm or power resulting from projecting the idea; knowing also comes from focusing only on what is noble and loving.

Mercury Retrograde in Virgo

(any or all of these may apply)

Here Mercury's energies slow down to rethink in an analytical mode. The mind here becomes a critic of all it sees, and judges the practical usefulness of every idea and every approach. "A place for everything, and everything in its place"—including ideas, actions, and feelings. This position continually analyzes place and function using check lists, and reviews everything to evaluate its perfection. This one worries about old business in case it might happen again. Mercury here sees linkages between life areas when the health of one affects the other, as it is able to see the whole picture from a creative perspective. This is the servant seeing what another needs to hear, or heal. There may be a close and intimate understanding of animals, and how they communicate, or the ability to talk to animals. There may be vacillation about forms of perfection, or a critical unconscious intolerance. This position categorizes things in an unusual way, which may result in a filing system that is perfectly ordered, but makes no sense to anyone else. This position reminds others of facts to make perceptions more practical or realistic, and is willing to discuss anything to make it more perfect.

Mercury in Virgo is in its own 1st sign: Here discrimination is the quality of the mind, and differentiation the source of self-identity. Here the mind adjusts to a more proper conception of self within any process. *Mercury in its own 4th sign* offers practical application as the grounding, taproot, or platform of ideas. Here the mind's base of operation is how it discerns and compartmentalizes. *Mercury retrograde in Virgo* multiplies, analyzes, and compartmentalizes to establish its widest base, and ideas are grounded in how they were applied in the past.

Personalities: The accountant, subcontractor, public health worker, veterinarian, medical researcher, animal trainer or handler, social reformer.

Knowledge comes from the adjustments that lead to order, or "the work" being furthered; knowledge also comes from seeing the place and function of any given idea or piece of information.

Mercury Retrograde in Libra

(any or all of these may apply)

Here Mercury's energies slow down to rethink in an aesthetic mode. Here the mind weighs everything, reduces the extremes, and sees ideas from the side that naturally opposes, counters, or balances the information or premise. In this sign the mind filters all it surveys through aesthetic judgments; these may be based in unrealistic abstractions, or may be eternal ideals or standards of measurement. This position can name the timeless example, or communicate the transfigured vision, that helps to adjust others' visions, perspective, standards. There may be the light touch of a graceful communication style, or lightweight thinking because of superficiality. This position sees the equality or similarities in everyone. There may be vacillation due to unconscious adjustment to another's ideals, or adjusting the point of view to what seems most agreeable to another. Often the perspective changes about old relational experiences. This is a friendly and agreeable communication style that fills in others' gaps and communicates a different aesthetic. This position is able to rationally communicate some reconstructed ideal, or give others a new ideal. This is the position of the mature, elegant, and gracious mind, or point of view.

Mercury in Libra is in its own 2nd sign: Here the level of refinement confirms its own worth. There is a constant weighing of alternatives to try to establish stability, and a striving to see the beautiful essence and naturalness of anything. *Mercury in its own 5th sign* holds that balance is the natural expression of judging and comparing multiple points of view. Here graceful initiatives refine any form by judging its naturalness. *Mercury retrograde in Libra* is the mind refining its observations before expressing itself.

Personalities: The judge, actor, marriage counselor, art critic, interior designer, archeologist, moralist.

Knowledge comes through dancing with the oscillation and finding the balance; knowledge also comes from observing the difference between what is central and what is peripheral.

Mercury Retrograde in Scorpio
(any or all of these may apply)

Here Mercury's energies slow down to rethink in a reform mode. In this position the mind intensely destroys previously held conceptual forms. Hidden things are ferreted out, and sexuality, power, life, death, loss, and the nature of opportunity are constantly questioned. There are fantasies around what might be, if certain conditions were fulfilled. There may be repetitious negative thinking, or reiteration of other's negative ideas. Here the mind seeks to find the path to the truth behind forms; it drills ever deeper, and may find gold, oil, or garbage. Mercury here is never satisfied with superficialities, and it is relentless in the pursuit of whatever will lead to completion. This position takes a new look at what was discarded. There may be an unusual feeling-understanding of some desire, or sudden insights into another's subconscious values. This position instinctively spots self-destructive behavior or mental-verbal evasions, and has the ability to pierce through others' defenses. There may be power struggles within the mind, with one point of view trying to destroy all others. This relentlessly pursues understanding the subconscious. There may be endlessly repeating secretive thoughts. This is the verbal executioner, searching for inconsistencies in others.

Mercury in Scorpio is in its own 3rd sign: Here power and desire are constantly exploring, intensely pursuing and gathering information. Old illusions may be desired anew. *Mercury in its own 6th sign* indicates a placement where the mind constantly self-adjusts to practical exigencies, and uses power and desire to alter situations. Here the mind explores final adjustments before bringing any given idea or approach to the surface. *Mercury retrograde in Scorpio* offers the ability to "cut to the chase" once hurtful speech and attitudes have been overcome.

Personalities: The swordsman, detective, medical researcher, war historian, religious reformer, satirist, inquisitor, spy, policeman, cryptographer.

Knowledge comes through piercing the form and feeling the depth; knowledge also comes from seeing what of value must be reclaimed from the past.

Mercury Retrograde in Sagittarius

(any or all of these may apply)

Here Mercury's energies slow down to rethink in a visionary mode. The mind seeks truth through opening to the universals in any given idea or learning. There are pronounced spiritual-moral inclinations, leading the mind to judge all input relative to previously held standards. Ever-expanding scattering possibilities may be brought into every discussion and consideration. Timeless messages are received or given; here the inspired mind surveys possibilities and shares these with others. There is a tendency to go in a thousand directions, all within the mind, resulting in distractions and deflections. Mercury here searches for truth, hoping it will be recognized by some old part of self. Old truths may be stated in new ways for future examination. This position focuses on everywhere but here, and every time but now. All standards are seen to be true, all morality is considered valid, and all options are left open. This position has the ability to name the truth behind another's restlessness, argues cases to further all truth, but is extremely distractible. There is a need to focus on the highest, to teach unusual spiritual points of view. The mind speaks frankly, but not necessarily in a direct or focused way, which can result in abstract judgments signifying nothing. There may be indirect honesty. Often the left hand doesn't know (or care) what the right hand is doing. This position is sincere, but may be impatient and restless due to a lack of discipline.

Mercury in its own 4th sign: Here truth is its own basis, and vision is its own foundation. This is the future as it is grounded in the present, and an abundant view of possible ways to fulfill needs. This position finds security in knowing how to deflect or run away from anything. *Mercury in its own 7th sign* regards truth as its own judge, balance, and filter. There may be perspectives on other moralities and approaches to truth from other times and cultures. Here the mind seeks others for the rhythmic give-and-take of free flowing ideas. *Mercury retrograde in Sagittarius* is the non-possessive idealistic mind seeking opportunities to explore truth so it can grow in social effectiveness.

Personalities: The preacher, mentor, visionary, humorist, satirist, religious reactionary, judicial scholar, philosopher-historian, professional sportsman or woman.

Knowledge comes from inspiration and vision; knowledge also comes from serving the highest truth and good for the sake of the future.

Mercury Retrograde in Capricorn

(any or all of these may apply)

Here Mercury's energies slow down to rethink in an organizational, utilitarian mode. The mind searches for that which brings power, authority, recognition, and/or effectiveness. This position looks at various forms of government, law, and order to find unshakable arguments. There may be discussions regarding disciplines, self-imposed rules, limits, or chains of thought. Mercury here teaches others about the nature of personal power and responsibility, and pragmatically reviews structures, or how things are put together or organized. There may be heavy speech, chronic pessimism, or mental-verbal power struggles based in unconscious fears. Here the responsible view is expressed, or another's words are spoken in a responsible manner. This position sees the powerful in their blindness or obtuseness. It may speak assertive subconscious demands, express authority indirectly, or remind others of their responsibilities. This position knows how to concentrate to find the unsuspected, and speaks in a dignified way that compels others' attention. There is a sensitivity to conservative ideas from other times, or other people, and the ability to rethink conventional points of view and what is behind them.

Mercury in Capricorn is in its own 5th sign: Here authority sees itself as the only authentic form of self-expression. This is the willful mind's power play justifying its dictates. This position has the ability to play as it fulfills its duty. *Mercury in its own 8th sign* offers authority as a form of power, magnetism, limitation, transcendence, and reorganization as a regenerative force. *Mercury retrograde in Capricorn* knows that unsuspected possibilities can be seen through reviewing past responsibilities.

Personalities: The diplomat, ambassador, corporate policy-maker, one who speaks on behalf of authority.

Knowledge comes from the utilitarianness of information; knowledge also comes from ideas crystallized into forms of power.

Mercury Retrograde in Aquarius

(any or all of these may apply)

Here Mercury's energies slow down to rethink in a synthesizing mode. In this sign the mind searches for concretized ideals, or ideas about world or social service. It seeks friends as sounding boards. The mind synthesizes ideas, then recombines the possibilities into newer, different syntheses. Mercury here seeks a universal vision by looking within holistically. This position furthers work that was started by another. It seems able to see and know things from a different space and time continuum.

Here old ideals are given new applications. There may be new insights into old friends, or old ambitions, or a new look at old values sustaining one's sense of honor. Here abstractions are made to serve subconscious urges. There is mental brilliance from drawing on unsuspected details, resulting in a synthesized, detached, or dispassionate overview. This position sees others' expressions impersonally, and is friendly in speech because of sensitivity to other's unvoiced perceptions. Mercury here sees longterm contributions to be made, and has insights into managing others' energies. This is the resourceful mind judging from the highest ideal, offering new applications of old principles.

Mercury in its own 6th sign: This position makes practical adjustments through synthesis. Discussion of ideals is seen to be a form of service, as it prepares the abstract mind to search for practical applications of truth. *Mercury in its own 9th sign* gives the power of synthesis as a truth expressing itself through an integrated vision. Here a stabilized higher vision is offered to others. *Mercury retrograde in Aquarius* sees world service as a truth.

Personalities: The inventor, world-server, spokesperson for a group, computer guru, brilliant charismatic, electromagnetic pioneer, innovator or renovator.

Knowledge comes from seeing the unified vision; knowledge also comes from experiencing one's ability to contribute as a builder of the culture.

Mercury Retrograde in Pisces
(any or all of these may apply)

Here Mercury's energies slow down to rethink in a movie-watching or witness mode. It is over-attracted to the past and possesses an unsuspected gentle sensitivity; it watches the endings. This position indicates an intuitive mind, but it is never quite sure of what it is seeing, hearing, or knowing. There may be visions from the distant past, as information is constantly coming in from the collective consciousness or Collective Unconscious. This position is highly receptive to subtle signals from the subconscious, whether one's own or another's. There may also be a lack of clarity about the meaning of these signals, resulting in ambivalence and frustrating the ability to act decisively. There may be a feeling of being lost in a fog, pressure drops into sorrow, or confusion through addiction to confusion. Here the mind shifts in empathy with its environment. Sometimes things are remembered that never happened, or which happened to another. This is the position of the compassionate mind, or the hypocrite able to justify anything because of seeing things from multiple viewpoints. Mercury here is able to become a living conscience witnessing the universal human experience. There may be compassionate speaking of what another needs to hear, sensitivity to speaking others' conscience, or self-deceit through confused standards. This position reasons instinctively, sees whole situations, but may not be able to communicate satisfactorily. Mercury here witnesses the end of old ghosts, in self and others, is able to speak for all time, but may be hurt too easily. Here there is an atmospheric sensitivity and an environmental impressionability. This position may offer the gift of visionary poetry, and uses a subtle sense of humor to communicate universal truths.

Mercury in Pisces is in its own 7th sign: Here compassion is a constant self-renewing opportunity, and deceit a constant self-renewing judgment. Here one sees the equality of all beings and the universality of human experiences through all times. This position offers the opportunity to witness another's selfhood, or balance another's karma through offering alternatives. *Mercury in its own 10th sign* offers compassion as its own fulfillment and the culmination of the communication process, or deceitfulness as a quality which always shows itself publicly. *Mercury retrograde in Pisces* gives an awareness of universals, the ability to know and teach the true nature of personal responsibility, and if appropriate, the ability to mitigate another's karma.

Personalities: The nurse, smuggler, ambitious opportunist, "slacker," "power behind the throne," snitch, prayer group leader, philanthropist, mystic, director of institutions demonstrating high principles, spiritual teacher.

Knowledge comes from feeling the vastness around the immediate; knowledge also comes from passing on the truth to those who also serve.

5

MERCURY RETROGRADE IN THE HOUSES (NATAL, PROGRESSED, RETURN CHARTS, OR BY TRANSIT)

HERE WE WILL EXPLORE some possible manifestations of Mercury retrograde in the various houses. It holds as true for the progressed chart as the natal, and inferences may be drawn for the various return charts. I have written these paragraphs so they may also be applied to the transits. Not all of what is written about each house will come forth each time, but looking back over the life, it will become evident that at least one of the influences manifested each time Mercury retrograded in the house in question. The house in which transiting Mercury retrogrades provides important information about the areas of life in which revisions and revisitings will occur, in terms of a direct field of experience.

Should transiting or progressed Mercury move retrograde across two houses, or hit its station within the cuspal zone (the span of transition between two houses, using multiple house division systems simultaneously), the astrologer and client are offered unique insights into how these two areas of life are linked within the experience and consciousness. If we add the aspects[1] made by the stationary points to the natal, progressed,

---

[1] An aspect is a specific angular relationship between any two points in an astrological chart. The more commonly used aspects include the conjunction, sextile, square, trine, and opposition, with many minor ones too numerous to be named here. Each aspect has its own quality and meaning, and I consider aspects to be one of the four fundamental "building blocks" of astrology, along with planets, signs, and houses.

and various return chart planetary positions, much information can be gleaned about future attitudes in all areas of life and self. For a detailed explanation of the concept of stationary points, refer back to chapter 2.

One example of how to apply this is to focus attention to wherever the transiting Mercury retrograde stationary points fall, and note their aspects to the progressed Mercury. If the progressed positions indicate the unfolding of the potential shown in the natal chart, the transiting Mercury stations give an opportunity to reflect on how the life is understood as a progression of experience to this point, and how that experience is perceived and interpreted.

The aspects made by the Mercury stationary points to any other point in any chart indicate the relative challenges and opportunities of perceiving from a different point of view, and show the perceptions upon which the future span of experience will be approached. The aspects made by the stationary points to the natal positions show the evolving frame of reference around lifelong issues. Aspects to the progressed positions highlight the issues connected to the process represented by those planets. The aspects to the various return positions[2] indicate functional understandings or activities around the various natal and progressed issues and areas, relating to the time period the return chart represents. This may be extrapolated in many ways for the various charts.

Mercury Retrograde in the 1st House

(any or all of these may apply)

Here we see reflections on selfhood and self images, or the return of old ways you used to identify with, even if only indirectly or symbolically. During these periods you remember long-forgotten behavior patterns from earlier times in life; old instincts or subconscious reactions may surface. There are re-

---

[2] Return positions are the degree, sign, and house placement of the Sun, Moon, and planets in solar, lunar, and planetary return charts.

flections on old ways of knowing who you are and who you are not, taking into account subconscious factors not previously understood. With this position you see your unique purpose of being from a different point of view. Instincts and automatic behaviors can be viewed from a new perspective. There may be confusion about who you are and what you are here to do. Review how your "lens on the world" has been shaped, and change what you need to on the basis of current information, letting go of assumptions and prejudices.

Insights lead to new motivations about values and resources, new ambitions, new ideals to be explored, or new ways of "bringing the past to flower." Here looking at your past offers unusual insights into how you have structured your personality, and you are able to see new truths about personal authenticity. Prepare for future self-expression based on a new self-image, or glimpse different personal forms of play or art. This position offers regeneration of health on all levels, or the ability to see how subconscious issues have contributed to the degeneration of health. There could be new insights about how you are being equal or unequal in relationships, or how old patterns influence your ability to react to opportunities. Here there are practical adjustments around joint resources or values, or the collective value structure, leading to either regeneration or loss. You may experience the spontaneous expression of old truths in different forms, and have the ability to re-ground your authority in a new public form. This is a position of seeing how power—or how you appear to others—needs to be grounded in a new self-image, or how past self-images no longer satisfy what is needed for personal fulfillment. You can have new ideas and insights into goals, ambitions, and friendships, or find a new value in what used to motivate you. Here you receive insights into past limitations and restrictions, and understand the value or worthlessness of these. This is a time of looking back at new beginnings and recently completed endings, and identifying with the new as it is beginning to manifest. Revision how you see power, energy, and action.

Mercury Retrograde in the 2nd House

(any or all of these may apply)

This is a time of reflecting on old values. Look at what you have and how you use it. Old ways of making money may return, or you may get new insights into the worth of your assets. There may be misunderstandings about money. You may use the written or spoken word to create an alternate source of income, or may share your value system with others. See the inner resources that you draw on that sustain your self-image in different ways. This is a time to review old ideas about stability, and update the information. See the material objects you value in terms of their symbolic meaning and worth.

Insights can lead to new motivations in sibling relations, environmental sensitivity, and communications. A new ideal of security may present itself. You may have an insight into why you want the home you do, or a new way of seeing your parents' ambition for you, and its relationship to your values. Here you may go public with your art, your playfulness, or your spontaneity. This is a time where you could have a vision of future health or disease in the making. It may be a preparation phase for a different kind of work. You are now able to see how your values have contributed to the degeneration or regeneration of your relationships, or how your values-as-desire have attracted the relationships and opportunities you subconsciously wanted. This is a time for reflecting on how desires have been exteriorized; let go of outmoded values to regenerate. This position helps you adjust your values to actualize present truths; here you may see the truth behind old power or authority issues. Reflect on the roots of old friendship issues and the values underlying these; see how your values were influenced by past friendships. Here you gain insights into old limitations and motivations. This is a time for reviewing what you can draw on to sustain and empower the new cycle that began to unfold when Mercury crossed the Ascendant.

Mercury Retrograde in the 3rd House

(any or all of these may apply)

This is a time for new insights into old ways of interpreting sensory information, reprogramming your perceptual mechanism, or developing a new point of view on old information or ideas. Someone may lie to you about your environment, or you may receive unusual information about your environment—actual or psychic. Any curious, roundabout signals from your environment are not to be taken at face value. There may be possible misunderstandings with a sibling, or the return of an old issue between you, for good or ill. You may receive an insight into a sibling, or friend who is like a brother or sister to you. Find new ways of understanding what you know and how you know it, or new ways of interpreting situations. Important communications are delayed, or a communication is either forgotten or put on the back burner.

This is a time to review why you need what you need, or deal with ghosts regarding your feelings of security; it is time to review and close out old security issues. You may have new insight into ambitions for your children, or the subconscious workings of your children's friends. By looking at your work history, you see how far you can go working for another. There may be a return of an old ailment thought to be finished. Here you can review the truth of some relationship, or see subconscious patterns that you learned because of what a relationship symbolized abstractly. Receive insights into your personal magnetism, and why you want or do not want something. Review your losses, and see how you attracted what you needed to overcome some weakness. A truth or moral standard may manifest in a curious or roundabout way, or there may be an indirect assault on that truth. Gain new insights into the counterpoint of your philosophy, and review paradoxes in your vision. Practical adjustments may be necessary to better utilize some actualized position or power. Here you may adjust your understanding of why you exist, and see what needs to be sacrificed to expand your power or authority. You may now understand a friend's pleasures from a different point of view, or take a new look at your enthusiasm for a goal. Observe the basis of your sorrow, and review the foundations of your life. Communicate through imagery rather than forms, and see your issues of humanness differently, mobilizing a timeless view. This is a time for reviewing new discoveries, observing what is presenting itself, gathering information and communicating it, and exploring emerging possibilities involving others.

Mercury Retrograde in the 4th House

(any or all of these may apply)

This is a time for reflections on childhood, family, needs, roots, and security issues. Misunderstandings with a parent, or another family member, may take place. An infantile behavior pattern may return in some contemporary form, or you may receive an insight about this in another. Review the past, or renew an emotional response to something that indirectly symbolizes part of this past. You may remember an old feeling-thought, and gain new insight into it. You may see a parent in a different light, or gain an insight into an inherited family behavior pattern. Take a new look at an old need or security issue. See the circumstances of your nurturing and caring in a new light. Find new forms of contributing to the fulfillment of some immediate emerging need.

See what motivates your creativity. You may experience a sorrow connected with children, or some aspect of childhood. Examine why you inhibit your self-expression. Find new ways to achieve a work goal; see the plan differently. Examine health goals. Review how old relationships culminated, or see how a present relationship will culminate. Examine the truths behind why you want what you want. See past security issues and ideas as the basis of future degeneration or regeneration. You may gain new understanding about your truth, and how your truth attracts and repels various aspects of your life. See old losses as offering a new foundation of strength, and your needs as a magnetic force helping you move beyond old limitations. Take a new look at opportunities for personal flowering, or why you cannot utilize your position in life more effectively. You may sense how to adjust to better achieve your goals. You now can see friendships in a different light, and change the basis of your belief systems accordingly. There may be a spontaneous expression of sorrow, or a closure of some sort. Look for opportunities to communicate something about the eternal human experience. See love's sorrows differently. This is a time to review recent decisions, consolidate and secure your base, look back over a turning point, find your true family, and see what sustains and nourishes that which is unfolding.

Mercury Retrograde in the 5th House

(any or all of these may apply)

This is the time for a return of old playfulness. Review your style of self-expression and forms of play to get unusual self-awarenesses. Here the inward-turned mind explores unusual symbolic art forms, or receives insights into games. Question why you love what you love. Here you either waste time in scattered self-expression, or reveal your deep and subtle creative power. Tinker around the edges with your art or self-expression; explore alternative forms. Children may bring new insights about your own childhood issues, though there could also be misunderstandings or miscommunications with children. You may meet or re-meet someone who reminds you of your child (if you have one), or someone from your childhood. There may be a new insight into love, or the return of an old flame.

You can gain insights into what motivates your search for truth. See the limitations in your ability to adjust to circumstances. You may have insights into your goals in relationships, and may need to rethink why you want those relationships. Revise your expression of power. See how your weaknesses show themselves; this will show you why you must give up certain limitations. Use games or forms of play to regenerate. Here you receive new insights into where your truth is leading you, or the ethics of your morality. Review old losses of power, position, or authority, and reclaim your power by seeing why you had to give up these old forms. Play with the ebb and flow of power and authority from a different point of view. Opportunities may be derived from friendships and social groups seen in a different light. You can now understand why you seek to possess ideas, things, and people. Play with how you explore ideas and process information, and find new ways to learn and communicate. Find new ways to value your past and your history, for the worth of your ancestral background may become apparent. This is a time for looking back on the new base of operations and the emergences of the recent past. Renew and exteriorize power, and prepare to release the energy of the potential in a form authentic to self.

Mercury Retrograde in the 6th House

(any or all of these may apply)

This is a time for reflections about health, or for looking at indirect signals you may be getting about health. Review work done; you may get a signal about something yet to come in your work situation. There may be unusual insights into forms and ideals of practical spiritual service. Reflect on the motives of opponents, past or present. You may receive a curious insight from one who works for you, or a signal from within about something going on in the life of someone in your service. A pet comes into your life who reminds you of one you used to have. Remember an old technique needed for some new task at hand. See a different way to do a job efficiently.

You may receive flashes of insight about a child's values. Examine the worth of your personal style, or how your play reveals hidden subconscious values. Look at what motivates your relationships, or get closure on old relational business. See what limits your ability to respond to new opportunities. Reflect on your use or misuse of power, and the outcome of limitations voluntarily released. Perhaps there is the return of an old sports injury, or something incurred as a result of recreation. You may have interesting insights about the fulfillment of your truth, morality, higher learning; you may even adopt a different philosophy. You can now know the truth behind your quest for power and authority, and why you project the worldly image you do. You may get unusual insights into the morality or philosophy of a parent. Lost friends may return, or you may see the degeneration of a friendship from a different point of view. Look at the limitations of a friendship, or hindrances in your ability to make friends. This is a time to renew your goals, and abandon outmoded goals, friends, and ideals. Sorrow may come to the surface, along with an opportunity to end an old phase of life. Adjust your self-image, review the uniqueness of your work, and express your values spontaneously. Anchor ideas using alternative approaches and applications. Find a new way to see or communicate some need. Unusual insights into childhood or personal ancestry, or hidden factors in the family environment, may present themselves. This is a time of practical adaptation and adjustment before something comes to the surface, a time of learning and reviewing the place and function of what has individualized up to this point in the process. See the possible practical applications of power; prepare to take something public.

Mercury Retrograde in the 7th House

(any or all of these may apply)

This is a time for reviewing relationship issues. An old relationship may return, or you may be reminded of one from your past. Lost opportunities, or one that has been on hold, may come back into sight. Observe how your business or marriage partner perceives him- or herself, or how this person's self-image is influenced by subconscious or collective consciousness factors. There may be miscommunications with partners, or misunderstandings about marriage and relationships. There may be a return of that which opposes you. Review lost opportunities, or return to the opportunities most suited to you after you review a previous growth cycle.

Value your work from a different point of view. Wealth may be derived from pets in a roundabout way. There may be a second chance to communicate love or affection. See different artistic approaches or get the picture of what a form of play is all about. You may have unusual views about needs, early family life, or distant ancestry. Ideas may come from the grandparents, whether they are present or not. Thoughts about what motivates self-destructive behavior, and unusual or roundabout ways to close these out, may be on your mind. See how limiting your options focuses your power in self-regenerative ways. Find friends who share your truth, or become a spokesperson for some group that shares your philosophy. Rethink your truth or morality; understand how your honor will ultimately show itself. See the truth or morality of a friend from a different point of view; find a new way to express your goals. Understand a group philosophy from a different angle, or how your life myths have degenerated. See the self-destructiveness of your old motives, and find regenerative strength in renewing your self-understanding from a broad and timeless point of view.

Review how you or another behaved or communicated in an old relationship, as seen from the other's point of view. Put your values or resources to use in a different way; adjust your values by adopting new information coming in. You may spontaneously express new ideas, or old ideas may express themselves in new forms more appropriate to who you have become. Play with ideas, or communicate in a playful way. Understand how ancestry may condition the way relationships fulfill themselves. This is a time to see how love is the ambition of all relationship, or how playfulness is a goal to be embraced within some relationship. Take a new look at how a person's truth motivates or hinders his or her ability to respond to opportunity. This is a time to reflect on what has surfaced, take a different look at the ideal, and reconstruct whatever is needed to embrace the archetype revealing itself.

Mercury Retrograde in the 8th House

(any or all of these may apply)

This is a time to review your current desires, or you may experience the return of a past desire. Examine degenerative or regenerative behavior in yourself or another. Messages may come from the dead, or you may be remembering those who are long gone. Examine how you accepted an idea or point of view from one who is no longer in your life. Find new applications for an idea from someone who lived in a different era. Understand power from a different perspective. Review your past; see how you have grown beyond old limitations, and reflect on how you have changed your ideas, or need to do so now. Take a new look at a partner's values, or society's values. Get a new perspective on the power you have reclaimed from your losses.

See what motivates your search for truth. Get new insights into the use of power, and see how your misuse of power caused past sorrows by betraying your truth or philosophy. Find a new motive for a new future. Review your professional goals, and if appropriate, make new ones. You may be helped professionally by a new friend who reminds you of an old one, or you may remember an old friend, and how his or her authority or position in life either destroyed or empowered this person. Find the power and desire to close an outmoded truth. Review your use or misuse of personal magnetism; see how you have attracted what you desired. Examine the imprecisions in your past thought-forms. Here you can see loss and gain from a different perspective. You may receive new information about wealth, as seen from a social perspective. Adjust your communication style, or rethink the effectiveness of your ideas, given practical exigencies.

You may find yourself playfully expressing some childhood trait, some inherited pattern, or enjoying a parent in a new way. See a parent's self-expression from a new point of view. Understand how your desires may be related to a parent. Observe your artistry and playfulness; take a new look at your need for play and self-expression. An idea connected to work or your practical skills may return. Play with different points of view or new information. You may have a new vision of spiritual effectiveness, or previously held ideas about the truths of life and self may present themselves anew. Reflect on how relationships come apart because power is misused. This is a time to review the potential apart from the actualized form; let go of old ideas about what is desirable, what is needed, and see what is obsolete. Look back over the emerging ideal, get a different view of what is valuable, and focus your faith.

Mercury Retrograde in the 9th House

(any or all of these may apply)

This is a time to review your philosophy, morality, and concept of truth. See ethics differently, taking into account overlooked details and paradoxes. Take a new look at your future, or other ways your future might unfold. This is a time to travel to distant lands, literally or figuratively. Use imagination to teach, or explore subtleties of larger truths. You may choose to re-educate yourself; this can free your abstract mind from obsolete concepts. You may understand new applications of old philosophies. See how different philosophies and religions express the same truths, or how similar philosophies and religions have multiple or different truths. You may distribute ideas of truth and freedom through some form of media, including subconscious suggestion. You may send or receive messages from "far away" in space or time, or receive ideas from Divine Mind.

Embrace different ways of seeing truth as the substance of desire, or how desire concretizes itself. Here ultimate ideals may be glimpsed, and truths about justice embraced. Find equals who are friendly toward your truth. See new ways to communicate in relationships, or new perceptions about unconscious factors in relationships. Review the sources of your moral-spiritual existence; take a new look at your truths, and adjust what needs to change. There may be the return of an old health issue, or you may "get to the bottom" of same. Review how much you did or did not play with your children, or how you did or did not inhibit their free expression. See how you have inhibited your artistic expression or your most authentic self; review artistic methods, forms of recreation, and subconscious patterns. Observe your past differently for purely practical reasons, freeing yourself from fear, egocentricity, and obsolete habit patterns. Make philosophical adjustments because new needs have arisen, or because of domestic reasons. Confused or visionary ideas may come forth.

You may have opportunities to speak what you should have spoken long ago. Review how old ideas fit a new truth. You may experience a regeneration of your values, find a new power or potential in some asset, or receive a signal that makes you reflect on lost resources or an old unstable value structure. See your self-image differently, reconsider a vision of your future, glimpse the why of your timelessness, or prepare to learn or re-learn something greater. This position brings the culmination of sorrow, or something needing closure; here you accept the authority to bring something to an end. See a friend's ambition differently, or see the true goals of some group. Observe how various understandings of truth motivate all quests for power and position. Here the search for freedom motivates one's personal authority, and closes old forms of social power. This is a time of broad-visioned looking back on the spiritual harvest of what is culminating from multiple spiritual revelations. Revise your ideas of truth accordingly.

Mercury Retrograde in the 10th House

(any or all of these may apply)

This is a time for the return of some honor or position. Rethink forms of personal power and recognition and reconsider how you want to be seen by others. Old responsibility and control issues may arise. Be alert to the subconscious patterns in public situations. Speak for some governmental authority, or for the power structure of some group. See government reports from a different point of view as a result of knowing different information. Understand your profession as it is seen through others' eyes, take into account unusual points of view, and value different ways of performing the same task. Teach using different methods, tools, perspectives, or unconventional imagery.

Explore alternative ways to confirm your truth, observing your need for control from a different angle. See the value in a different future. Communicate a desire indirectly; glimpse new ways of communicating power. Take a different approach to how you perceive gain and loss; this can lead to new ways of responding to opportunity. Find a new way to understand and approach opportunities from your past. Review past relationships and see anew what your power, authority, and control issues were, and how these were the foundation of any conflict between the actual and the ideal. If possible, play at being more spontaneous publicly in ways that will improve your health and truth of being. Recreate your path of truth, your spiritual expression, or use some structure or plan to adjust toward a more authentic self-expression. Childhood issues can now be seen in a different light. Different information about your subconscious need for power provides opportunities to balance your foundations of character, and helps you understand how some of your ambitions are the result of earlier, misunderstood behavior patterns. Here you can understand how attachment to forms degenerates or regenerates ideas and patterns of learning; crystallizations can now be perceived as limiting the magnetism of ideas.

Rethink the meaning of ambition, authority, and public influence in your personal life and self-image. Here you can see how ambition, values, and motive are related, and how anyone's public standing is ultimately determined by the problems lurking within the unconscious. Your quest for honor, authority, or power may now be seen as motivating your ambition, and what groups you are involved in. This is a time to review how this cycle of activity has culminated, and reflect on the purpose of your aspiration. You can now have new insights into how your truth has been concretized in a form of power, as well as the true worth of whatever has been fulfilled.

Mercury Retrograde in the 11th House

(any or all of these may apply)

This is a time when friends may return, or you may see the subconscious of a particular friend differently. Old friends are remembered, or new friends are made who seem like old ones. Look back at friendship patterns, and compare them to your ideal of community. You may also glimpse hidden factors in a friendship, or something of the nature of friendship itself. An old ambition may return, or you may remember an old dream. Here your hopes and ambitions can be seen from a different perspective. You may experience a different understanding of social expression, world service, or a group you are in. You get an alternative view of some old expectation, or receive a reward thought to be lost. This may be an indirect reward, or one that comes from roundabout means.

You may now receive business assets after a delay, or see how to use business assets differently. Seek to understand a parent's values through subconscious information, or indirect communication. You may develop different ideas about how to communicate truth, or receive indirect signals about the ethics of a situation, especially with a friend or a group. Understand what needs to be lost, or what needs to be gained, to further an ambition. You may see a way to ground your magnetism, or end an old limitation. Find a new way to play with your partner or another who balances you; express yourself spontaneously within a relationship. Make a practical adjustment to improve your health. Someone may appear to help you move toward a new work or health routine. If necessary, adjust your goals or group relations because of work, health, or your personal truth.

Indirect signals may come up regarding a pet's health. An opportunity returns for you to express your art, spontaneity, or authenticity. See a child's marriage partner in a different light. Find ways to see childhood losses as opportunities to move beyond a limitation. Rethink the loss of a parent, or see the loss of innocence from a new perspective. You may have memories of the collective values you were exposed to as a child. See the greater vision of an idea in an unusual way, or how any idea may be communicated from different perspectives. See the moral-spiritual ideal of a sibling from his or her point of view, or why a sibling has the ideal of truth he or she does.

This position offers the culmination of your value system, and your potential for world service may be seen. Look at how your present and past self-images could have fulfilled themselves differently. Check out the value of compassion. Goals, ideals, and friendships may now be seen as motivators of compassion or self-undoing. This is a time for harvesting the seed of what is yet to come. Look back on how this cycle has fulfilled itself. This is a time for seeing how to manage your energies differently, through reflecting on why you wanted what you wanted, and why you received what you received.

Mercury Retrograde in the 12th House

(any or all of these may apply)

This is a time to see roundabout ways to achieve closure. Here you can understand how your communication style causes you sorrow. The memories of the past echo; you may need to use indirect means to deal with your recurring ghosts. This position offers visions of the past and future that often overlap, and there may be possible confusion as to which is which. Here you receive glimpses into common ground issues of humanity, but you may confuse the ideas from collective consciousness with your own. This is a time for seeing cause and effect from a wider view. There may be activity behind the scenes, with intrigues and secrets that may never see the light of day (and if they do, the whole story will never be known). Understand your paradoxes and search for a way to communicate in a subtle or indirect manner. Reflect on the life movie that is ending; it is time to mythologize the cycle that has just completed itself. Look back on it as an experiment, observing everyone's motives.

Observe what motivates your self-image, and how your ability to achieve closure here conditions what will be presented in the new cycle approaching. Sorrow here is the harvest of values that were inappropriate; beware of clinging to objects and people. Closure here allows you to know the true worth of any thing or person. You can find insights about how ideas present themselves in your (and others') subconscious mind, and how perception and motivation are related. You can also observe how egocentricity and clinging to the past create sorrow. Review the unfinished business of your past to find the source of your power, or why things have degenerated. See personal magnetism differently; you can now understand how sorrow magnetically affects your children as well as the degeneration or regeneration of your authenticity and spontaneity. If needed, take a new look at old health issues, old work issues, or old spiritual issues. Adjust your relationships as you outgrow old motives, and remove subconscious blocks in communication. Adapt to greet new opportunities by being more spontaneous in your self-expression. Comprehend how your public self is perceived by others in indirect ways.

Explore your subconscious motives to get to the bottom of your truth; see your past moral standards in a new light, or from another's perspective. Understand why you value your ambitions, and anchor your future by adjusting your motives. You may have new ideas about power, authority, or influence; use indirect means to communicate your ambition. A superior may communicate to you in a way that creates insecurity or even closure. Examine your conscience, take a new look at which friends you value, and confirm your relationships with your good and true friends. This is a time for dividing, separating, and saying good-bye. Here you prepare for the future cycle by taking one last look back at what is rapidly ending, and receive the rewards you are due, for better or worse. You now have a chance to glimpse messages from Divine Mind about what has ended, and what part you played from a different perspective. You may receive signals about your unique function within the Universal chord of consciousness. Here you know what you must end, and what you must incorporate into your inner self, so you can learn a future role.

6

MERCURY RETROGRADE PERIODS AND HOW THEY INFLUENCE THE DIFFERENT SIGNS

MERCURY RETROGRADE periods influence people in different ways. For some, it may be the return of a lost opportunity; for others, their computers may crash. Mercury's rulership of the areas of the natal chart (or even the solar return, for that matter) can give us hints as to what area of our lives will be affected during the three (or four) times a year the transit occurs. Of course, the natal Mercury position, the progressed Mercury position, and the house the specific transit falls in also must be taken into consideration for a more detailed interpretation.

For Sun in Aries or Aries Ascendant

(any or all of these may apply during a Mercury retrograde period)

A relative may be seen in a new light. There may be a renewal of an old point of view, and communications are not what they seem. Short journeys do not turn out as expected, or a journey is canceled for unanticipated reasons. An actual or symbolic brother or sister may return. There may be a change in the environment, or something in the environment is seen in a different way. An old idea may be understood from a totally different interpretation. Discussions may not turn out as expected. An old health concern may return, or there may be a renewal of a health discipline. Previous job skills are needed in a new way, or context. Something about to surface in the public realm may necessitate personal adjustments. You may glimpse an equal's moral-spiritual truth, subconscious motives, or the source of his or her self-undoing. Expressing your values, confirming them through discussions, and seeing what grounds your perceptions are all issues. Achieve closure of old needs, or perhaps subconscious needs may surface. You may see a new way to confirm your creativity so you can further its ultimate realization. Rethink how you want your path of spiritual fulfillment to culminate. You can claim power from your losses, past and present, and glimpse some truths about your profession, or renew your ambitions. There may be discussions of ideas that oppose previously held truths. Here you can touch the foundations of your fears, and find the antidotes to them.

During any Mercury retrograde period, you need to review old ideas, see them differently, and make adjustments to further efficiency.

Meditation

I see my life as a many-faceted, interconnected whole. I am willing to adapt my understanding to better serve my work. All I learn and all I perceive is leading me toward a new view of my most effective practical path of truth and service. My insights are leading me to a deeper sensitivity and an ability to break up stagnant feelings.

For Sun in Taurus or Taurus Ascendant

(any or all of these may apply during a Mercury retrograde period)

Old values need to be reconsidered. An old debt returns, one that may have been forgotten. An old love may be remembered. There may be a chance to be creative or playful in ways long neglected (as in renewing an interest in a sport not played in years). There is a possibility of meeting someone who reminds you of a childhood friend, or you may meet a child who reminds you of another child in another time. You can see the basis of what you value, and why. Be careful of self-sabotage in discussions, through excessive worry or criticism. See the worth of your upbringing or family in a new light, get an insight into a child's profession or honor, or understand self-destructive health issues. Find a practical task to help your future dreams come true. There may be a spontaneous expression of nobility, or the loss of honor. You can get glimpses into the needs of friends or their partners. Look at a partner's ambition, find an opportunity to regenerate, or end a destructive pattern. This is a time to see what you are unresolved about, so you can close one thing as a preparation for opening another.

During any Mercury retrograde period you need to stop repetitive conversations with yourself and others about money, and take time to play or be creative.

Meditation

I am willing to learn to see resources and what I value differently. All I seek to possess gives me information that helps me know myself. I am learning to express my spontaneity and creativity differently, and what I receive gives me new self-worth. My insights are leading me to a new maturity, responsibility, and effectiveness.

For Sun in Gemini or Gemini Ascendant

(any or all of these may apply during a Mercury retrograde period)

You will have sudden, unusual insights into yourself, giving you a different perspective on some habit, self-image, or behavior, as it might be seen by another. You may remember something about your early life conditioning that leads to an insight into how and why you became who and what you are. An understanding can present itself unexpectedly in a new context helping you confirm an early life experience. You may go to a place, within yourself or in the world, that reminds you of your childhood. You may have an insight about a part of yourself that is related to the parent of the opposite sex, or a grandparent. Beware of returning to old values out of fear, and expressing them indirectly. You may have a glimpse into a child's truth, moral-spiritual focus, subconscious motivation, or self-undoing behavior. There may be the death of a pet during these periods. Examine your partner's honor. You can know how true a desire is for you, as well as how much you are willing to adjust to achieve it. Let go of obsolete truths, and renew your power in order to regenerate a future you thought was lost. Your spontaneous expressions can show you a deeper truth. This may be a time to end an old profession, or a professional enemy may surface in an indirect way. You may have roundabout discussions with friends, or see curious setbacks or reversals in a friend's work. Look at your ambition from a different angle, and make adjustments. Look back over how things have ended throughout your life.

During any Mercury retrograde period you need to review how you have diffused energy in the past rather than focused it, and rethink why you need to present so many faces to the world. Go back to the past to get a different point of view or a second opinion.

Meditation

With every new day I am receiving new information about my multifaceted talents and needs. I see my past differently in order to know better who I am. My confusion is leading me to get grounded so that I may flower more effectively. My insights are leading me to a wider, more compassionate vision that I can communicate with humor and goodwill.

For Sun in Cancer or Cancer Ascendant

(any or all of these may apply during a Mercury retrograde period)

This is a time to glean insights into your motivation, into some unproductive behavior, or some ending that needs to be achieved. You can see new ways to close old neglected life business, or you will have a chance to end something that should have ended before, but was postponed. Perhaps you will have an insight into a brother or sister. A signal may come in from the environment that should not be ignored, but should also not be taken at face value. Ideas are flowing from the subconscious to the brain-mind mechanism. You may understand how something you value can contribute to a larger goal. You can also see how a certain attitude or mode of expression contributes to your self-undoing. Take a new look at the sorrow of your childhood by seeing it from a larger point of view. It is a time to regenerate an old creative skill, or understand how your creativity can contribute in a larger way within a group. These are times when your work can fulfill itself. Opponents in the workplace may express themselves in peculiar ways. Get a new insight into a partner's truth, or their form of spiritual service. Power comes from a loss that leads to new spontaneity or creativity. A need may be fulfilled through some truth that presents itself. Communications may take place where honor is an issue, or an old issue may force you to adjust your sense of honor. Take a new look at group values, or hidden agendas in a friend's play. Be creative in order to achieve necessary closures.

During any Mercury retrograde period you need to address old dilemmas, paradoxes, or scatterings that paralyze action or create sorrow. Cease worrying over useless details while ignoring the larger picture.

Meditation

I now have a chance to close the parts of my past that I need to close. I see my motives from a different perspective, so I can communicate more effectively. I am learning to prioritize my thinking so my perceptions may serve a practical purpose. My insights are leading me to a noble, spontaneous, inspired understanding.

For Sun in Leo or Leo Ascendant

(any or all of these may apply during a Mercury retrograde period)

You may receive an insight into the hidden motives of a friend, or see a friend in a new light. An old friend may come back into your life. A friendship may begin or end. You may choose to renew a neglected goal or ambition. You may gain insight into a group you belong to. It is time to review self-sustaining inner worth issues, to reverse old values, or to change the way you use what you have. The money flow may slow down. You may need to rethink how you plan to achieve your goals. These are times when you may see or express a new truth, resulting in difficult discussions with another. You see family goals, or the way the family deals with loss and regeneration, differently. You see a child's talents flowering, or get an insight into a child's mate. You may gain insight into your future health, or ways to adjust toward alternative futures. You see a partner's desire, playfulness, or creativity differently, or understand how their values relate to your own. You may discuss issues around the practical applicability of morality or philosophy. Find ways to value your honor or profession in a different way. Find ways to end sorrow or self-undoing behavior.

During any Mercury retrograde period you need to stop worrying about money, and take a new look at your goals and friends.

Meditation

I see that my many noble ambitions serve the light of truth. I am receiving new insights about wealth, and worth, that I may serve more effectively. Examining my friendships gives me new information about what I value. My insights are leading me to a greater sympathy, so that I may feel the need of the moment.

For Sun in Virgo or Virgo Ascendant

(any or all of these may apply during a Mercury retrograde period)

This is a time to gain insights into your self-image. Rethink your life direction, profession, or what constitutes "honorable" behavior. There may be a renewed flowering of an aspect of your personality that has been neglected or forgotten. By examining your own behavior or attitudes, you may have an insight into the parent of the same gender, or a grandparent, and how you are like that person. Find new ways to view resources that do not cause you so much sorrow. Examine how your self-expression attracts the friends you have, or how your expression creates loss in your life. Find ways to honor your family.

You may now glimpse the truth behind your play or creativity, and see ways to adjust that truth. See how your health is related to your ability to play, and find ways to regenerate your health. You may see a partner's past differently, or recognize the subconscious factors in how they choose relationships. Find a new way to look at a loss. It is a time to confirm your truth, and creatively express it. See what motivates your ambition. Be aware of self-sabotaging discussions within a group. These are times when you harvest your karma.

During a Mercury retrograde period you need to stop worrying and being so nervous or high-strung. Find ways to resolve any problem or issue by using multiple approaches, each at the perfect time.

Meditation

Contradictory information shows me the way to break free from routines. The change of pace gives me a chance to change my life direction appropriately. I am being shown ways to broaden my perspective by using my intuition. My insights are leading me to a deeper relaxation, a better sense of humor, and greater truth and compassion.

For Sun in Libra or Libra Ascendant

(any or all of these may apply during a Mercury retrograde period)

This is a time to gain insights into old motives by noticing an overlooked detail. You may get a new perspective on things that have ended by understanding the details differently. These are times to receive new insights into the paradoxes of old truths, or seeing how an old truth has another side. Take a final look at an old cycle and see its usefulness in your evolution. The return of an old truth long forgotten, or closing out something that was true, is possible now. See the truth of your roots or needs from a different perspective, and make adjustments. You may find yourself spontaneously playing in a new way. Examine your spirituality, and find new opportunities to exteriorize it. A partner's work, or attitude, may take unexpected twists and turns. You may lose something you value; find creative ways to deal with this loss, or see the value in another loss from another time. A long-held desire may come to you in a round-about way, or it may be a time when self-destructive behavior culminates. You can gain new insight into a profession. You see the karma of your profession in a new light, which may lead you to ending it. You may meet a friend of a friend, or get a new look at what a friend values, or how this friend deals with money. Something thought to be lost may return, or your karma may reverse itself in strange ways.

During a Mercury retrograde period you need to see your most beautiful truth from a different perspective, and end whatever needs to end so you can stop worrying.

Meditation

I am glimpsing truths I have never seen before. I am seeing the practicality of my motives, and ending those which are too narrow or too critical. I embrace alternative futures, knowing my truth will reveal itself in the end. My insights are leading me toward a vision of how I can contribute to my society in a larger way.

For Sun in Scorpio or Scorpio Ascendant

(any or all of these may apply during a Mercury retrograde period)

This is a time for new insights into old friends, or perhaps old friends return. You may lose a friend, or a friend reveals an aspect of themselves you never saw before. Review the adjustments you have made to further a life goal. Reconsider how you do what you do. Review your ambitions regarding practical spiritual service. See how any personal lack of focus diffuses your power. Look at old limitations you have outgrown from a new perspective based on the growth that has transpired. Old desire or power issues are brought up by friends, or a friend brings up an old loss. Something lost may return. There could be unexpected confrontations with something that opposes your values; discuss truth, ethics, or forms of practical spiritual service, closing out what you need to. Remember a pleasure from your past. Take a new look at how you deal with loss, how loss is related to how you do or do not express your needs, and see why certain losses were necessary. Take a new look at your children's needs, or what their partners consider honorable. You can get needed information to fill in some health picture, or a reminder of a health plan you have neglected. Understand a partner's values in a new light. You can now see the contradictions in your morality. Professional allies return, or there are unexpected occurrences relating to business money, including delays, whether to or from you. It is a time to end old self-destructive ways, and gain insights into the truth or morality of your motivation.

During a Mercury retrograde period you need to examine the usefulness of your desires, see how you can serve a greater group good, and stop focusing on unnecessary arguments, within and without. Also try to see the good in every death, and the regenerative potential in every loss.

Meditation

I choose a different set of desires to fulfill a more useful set of ambitions. All my past losses have served my need to go beyond forms. I see my friends and goals as indicators of my health and the need of my self-regeneration. My insights are leading me to exciting new self-revelation and new initiatives in life.

For Sun in Sagittarius or Sagittarius Ascendant

(any or all of these may apply during a Mercury retrograde period)

It is time to review what you have been putting forth for social approval. This is the time to reconsider your life direction, your public image, and examine why you want power. You may see a new side of your partner, or a variation on an old one. There may be thoughts about previous mates, or the return of one, if only temporarily. There is a need for, or an actual slowdown in, communication with partners; use roundabout or nonverbal means, and greet each other equally. Adjust values; see the future of your financial situation. Playful discussions go everywhere (or nowhere); so do discussions about honor and authority. You may have insights into a grandparent or parent, or the foundations of an old family need. You may observe how children perceive or communicate, or the return of a child's old health complaint. You can now see the value of work differently, or find a way to play at your work. You have insights into a partner's family, past, or a need. Old partnership issues may return. You may experience the closure of old desires, or sorrow at old losses. You may participate in discussions about loss, or perceive loss differently. See the worth of your truth, or form a group that shares that truth. You may see power in unsuspected ways, leading you to reverse your life direction. The truth of a friendship is suddenly revealed, and some friendships may end due to a shift in how truth is viewed. Those who aid your self-destruction may arrive or depart. You can now regenerate your power by ending some self-destructive behavior pattern.

During a Mercury retrograde period you need to reexamine your greatest public potential, or career self, and stop deflecting so much in your partnerships. See it from their point of view, and be more discerning in what you put forth.

Meditation

All my relationships give me information about my honor, my past, and my needs. I am seeing new ways to organize and prioritize parts of my life to fulfill its purpose more effectively. All new opportunities serve to ground me in a universal perspective. My insights are leading me to a deep and broad compassion for all, so that I may forgive and be forgiven.

For Sun in Capricorn or Capricorn Ascendant

(any or all of these may apply during a Mercury retrograde period)

See your truth from a more practical point of view; examine the overlooked details of your philosophy. Messages may come from far away; thoughts return to an old vision. Seek the causes of your health problems, and renew an old health discipline. You may understand the usefulness of speech in a new way. You may now glimpse the future of your profession, or experience reversals in your business philosophy. Old work dilemmas may reappear, still with no solution, or you may redo work already done once before. There is a return or loss of money, or money comes in from your creative works. There may be the appearance of something that opposes your perceptions or ideas; it fulfills a need you have to see a paradox. You may see how to fulfill your needs, and what you must do to achieve that end. You may see a child's values differently, or have an insight into child's play that teaches a great truth. Get insights into how the way you express your truth affects your health. You see a friend's ambition, death, or loss in a new light. Be careful of self-destructive behavior in public. You can gain insight into how self-destructive behavior fulfills itself, with the ability to counter it.

During a Mercury retrograde period you need to serve the truth and the truth will serve you. Review mixed signals sent out in the workplace, or to your own body. Allow your wisdom to help you adjust to a paradox, even if it seems to put you in an inferior position.

Meditation

I see my work as the foundation of my truth and future, and my health as the flowering of my philosophy and morality. I welcome alternative views of effective practical spiritual service. I accept the spiritual adjustments that enable me to serve more effectively. My insights are leading me to a sweet, abundant and enjoyable life.

For Sun in Aquarius or Aquarius Ascendant

(any or all of these may apply during a Mercury retrograde period)

This is a time for a review or return of an old desire, power, or limitation. You will see the usefulness of an old hindrance. There may be a reversal in jointly held wealth. Possible events: the return of an old form of play or recreation, finding a creative work done in the past but forgotten, seeing a child in a different light. This is a time to play with words and ideas from a different perspective. You may remember an old loss, or an old love may return. There may also be a return of that which opposes your values, or a past asset is seen in a new light. Discussions take place with siblings; you can receive insights into their subconscious. There may be reversals in a sibling's work or health. Unexpected value may be found in the home or in the past, and new spontaneity comes from that reconnection. Seeing something different in a child's past, the return of a child, or a childhood issue may all be important now. There are indirect communications about health, or seeing how you are self-sabotaging your health in some indirect way. A partner's values may be seen in a new light. You see the subconscious factors in another's ambitions. A loss may culminate, and the power of regeneration reclaimed. You get glimpses into how your truth causes you sorrow, or see your truth in ways you never have before. Here you see some part of your future at a closure point, and can make adjustments. There may be discussions with allies and friends around possible loss of status and position. You will get insights into the paradoxes around your ambition. At these times spontaneity and playfulness either bring opportunities or hinder your ultimate goals.

During a Mercury retrograde period you need to get rid of obsolete forms, inner and outer, which hinder the power of your world-serving purpose. Review what power means to you, and find a multilevel form in which you may express it creatively and whole-heartedly.

Meditation

I welcome new ways to express myself spontaneously and playfully. I am willing to give up impractical desires so that my authenticity may come forth. I see play as the great regenerator, and my old losses as necessary so that I can find the power of my genuineness and creativity. My insights are leading me to a vision of my ideal life.

For Sun in Pisces or Pisces Ascendant

(any or all of these may apply during a Mecury retrograde period)

Old partners or old enemies may reappear in their power. Examine how and why you attract conflict. Yield to the practical necessities of partnership. There may be worry about partners, reversals in partnership, or old partnership issues may be brought up. Here you find that a second home or second living situation will not satisfy your need for variety. Indirect information about a partner's self-image comes your way. Take a new look at your past, or get a new insight into family. Old childhood dilemmas can be reconsidered, or there may be a need to deal with these again. Old childhood verbal-perceptual gamesmanship may reappear. You may understand your upbringing in a different light. There could be discussions about money or values, or expected adjustments to wealth. You may have insights into how a child communicates or sees things. See how subtle environmental influences act on children. You may observe a child's self-destructive behavior, or how he or she handles closure in an unusual way. Gain insights into the value of work routines. This is the end of a period of loss or regeneration, or a return to old collective values. You may find friends who share your truth, or share reflections on its social relevance. You are presented paradoxes to dance with, in order to complete your character development. You may glimpse pieces of the truth or morality of your ambition, or what completes the work plan to fulfill that ambition. You may hear of reversals in a friend's work, or a friend's old health complaint returns. Beware of allowing old self-destructive behavior to return; instead, regenerate your power. See how desire creates sorrow, and how playfulness and spontaneity form karma.

During a Mercury retrograde period you need to address the split at the bottom of your being, find two approaches to need fulfillment, and be more discerning in your battles and your partnerships.

Meditation

I welcome the paradox in order to find a larger vision and a greater sense of humor. I honor the truth in all my partners as well as my opponents, past and present. I review my past to better understand the adventure of my life. My insights are leading me to magnanimity and goodwill as I dance with a boundless and infinite understanding.

7

FAMOUS MERCURY RETROGRADE PEOPLE

THE FOLLOWING is a list of some well-known (and not so well-known) people through history who had Mercury retrograde at birth. It is obviously not a comprehensive list, but it may yield some interesting patterns nonetheless. Some people were born at either the stationary retrograde or direct points, and they are included in a separate table (page 112). I have included (SR) or (SD) to note this. This may or may not have showed itself in some obvious way in their lives, or perhaps the stationary quality manifested in a form not evident to others. I leave it to astrological students of psychology and history to enjoy some of the possibilities presented by these people for seeing Mercury retrograde in a new light. Harpo Marx and Nostradamus spring to mind as two interesting variations on the indirect communication style of a Mercury retrograde.

The names on this list were compiled from a variety of sources.[1] As with any list of this sort, there is some possibility of erroneous data. This is especially true with modern actors and actresses, as they often have publicists who shave off one to five years from their true age.

For those of you born under a Mercury retrograde, see if you can identify with some of the characteristics of those who

---

[1] See end of table for a list of references.

share your sign. Whether or not you have Mercury retrograde in your birth chart, I am sure you will discover many insights on your own even if you are not an astrologer.

These lists were assembled from

Associated Press, "Today in History" (New York: Associated Press, daily).

Stephen Erlewine, *The Circle Book of Charts* (Tempe: American Federation of Astrologers, 1979).

Marc E. Jones, *The Sabian Symbols in Astrology* (originally published by the Sabian Publishing Society, 1969; reprinted Santa Fe: Aurora Press, 1993).

Doris Kaye and Frank Cackavell, *Celebrities thru the Zodiac* (Tempe: American Federation of Astrologers, 1974).

Lois Rodden, *The American Book of Charts* (Tempe: American Federation of Astrologers, 1980; now published as *Astro-Data II*, revised edition published 1993). I used the original edition when I made this study.

Famous Mercury Retrograde People

NAME	MERCURY'S SIGN	YEAR	OCCUPATION
Michel Nostradamus	Capricorn	1503	Astrologer, Prophet
Cervantes	Libra	1547	Author
Sir Francis Bacon	Aquarius	1561	Philosopher, Statesman, Jurist, Author
Ben Jonson	Cancer	1573	Playwright, Poet, Actor
William Lilly	Taurus	1602	Astrologer, Physician
Richard Cromwell	Libra	1626	Son of Oliver Cromwell, Politician
Henry Fielding	Taurus	1707	Novelist
Sir Joshua Reynolds	Cancer	1723	Portrait painter
F. A. Mesmer	Taurus	1733	Hypnotist
Louis XVI	Virgo	1754	Politician, Monarch
John Jacob Astor	Cancer	1763	Entrepreneur
Meriwether Lewis	Leo	1774	Explorer
George Bryan ("Beau") Brummel	Gemini	1778	Dandy
Jean-Baptiste Corot	Cancer	1796	Artist, Painter
Auguste Comte	Aquarius	1798	Social philosopher
Alexandre Dumas	Cancer	1802	Author
Lady Lytton (Wife of Bulwer-Lytton)	Scorpio	1802	Wife of author
John Sutter	Pisces	1803	Pioneer
Frederic Chopin	Aquarius	1810	Composer
Robert Schumann	Cancer	1810	Composer
Robert Browning	Taurus	1812	Poet, Author

NAME	MERCURY'S SIGN	YEAR	OCCUPATION
Stephen A. Douglas	Aries	1813	Politician
Sir Isaac Pitman	Capricorn	1813	Shorthand inventor
Richard Henry Dana	Cancer	1815	Author, Attorney (pioneer of seamen's rights)
Prince Albert, Consort of Victoria	Virgo	1819	Politician, Ruler
Fredrich Engels	Sagittarius	1820	Writer, Founded communist philosophy
Sir Richard Burton	Aries	1821	Explorer, Adventurer, Author, Linguist
Feodor Dostoevsky	Sagittarius	1821	Novelist
Ernest Renan	Aquarius	1823	Religious writer, Historian, Linguist
Thomas Huxley	Taurus	1825	Biologist, Zoologist, Surgeon, Writer
Joseph Lister	Aries	1827	Pioneer of antiseptic surgery
Henrik Ibsen	Pisces	1828	Playwright, Father of modern drama
Horatio Alger	Capricorn	1832	Author
Gustave Paul Doré	Capricorn	1832	Artist, Illustrator of classics
William Morris	Aries	1834	Poet
John Wesley Powell	Aries	1834	Scientist, Ethnologist
Frederic Bartholdi	Leo	1834	Sculptor
Leo Delibes	Pisces	1836	Composer
Ramakrishna	Pisces	1836	Spiritual author, Mystic
Victoria Woodhull	Virgo	1838	Feminist pioneer, Writer, Lecturer, Adventuress

NAME	MERCURY'S SIGN	YEAR	OCCUPATION
Henry George	Virgo	1839	Social reformer, Editor, Printer
Bret Harte	Virgo	1839	Author (short stories)
Emile Zola	Aries	1840	Novelist
Edward VII	Sagittarius	1841	Politician, Ruler
Camille Flammarion	Pisces	1842	Scientist, Author
Adelina Patti	Aquarius	1843	Opera singer
Abdul Baha	Gemini	1844	Mystic
Sara Bernhardt	Libra	1844	Actress
George Carey	Virgo	1845	Occultist
Daniel Burnham	Leo	1846	Architect of Skyscraper, City planner
Joseph Pulitizer	Aries	1847	Publisher
Wyatt Earp	Pisces	1848	Marshall, Outlaw
Luther Burbank	Aquarius	1849	Naturalist, Scientist, Botanist
Joseph Joffre	Capricorn	1852	Engineer, French WW I General
Edwin Markham	Taurus	1852	Poet
Albert Edelfelt	Leo	1854	Artist
Pope Benedict XV	Scorpio	1854	Pope
Percival Lowell	Pisces	1855	Astronomer, Scientist
Elbert Hubbard	Cancer	1856	Publisher, Editor, Essayist
H. Rider Haggard	Gemini or Cancer	1856	Novelist
Oscar Wilde	Libra	1856	Author

NAME	MERCURY'S SIGN	YEAR	OCCUPATION
Le Petomane (Joseph Pujol)	Gemini	1857	Unique entertainer
Sir Edward Elgar	Gemini	1857	Composer ("Pomp and Circumstance")
Pope Pius XI	Gemini	1857	Pope
Alan Leo	Leo	1860	Astrologer
Annie Oakley	Leo	1860	Cowgirl, Sharpshooter
Dorothy Dix	Scorpio	1861	Journalist who pioneered "Advice to Lovelorn" column
Arthur Laurie	Scorpio	1861	Chemist, Scientist
Charles Schwab	Pisces	1862	Industrialist
Auguste Lumiere	Scorpio	1862	Inventor, Scientist
Edward Bok	Libra	1863	Magazine editor, Writer
George Washington Carver	Gemini	1864	Botanist
Rudyard Kipling	Sagittarius	1865	Author
Gutzon Borglum	Aries	1867	Sculptor of Mt. Rushmore
Arturo Toscanini	Aries	1867	Conductor
Maxim Gorky	Pisces	1868	Novelist
Thomas Maybank	Aquarius	1869	Artist
Emma Goldman	Cancer	1869	Anarchist, Publisher
Alfred Adler	Aquarius	1870	Psychotherapist
Jan Christian Smuts	Gemini	1870	Author, Politician, Philosopher
Christian Morganstern	Taurus	1871	Poet
Alexander Scriabin	Capricorn	1872	Composer
Aubrey Beardsley	Virgo	1872	Artist, Caricaturist

NAME	MERCURY'S SIGN	YEAR	OCCUPATION
Max Beerbohm	Virgo	1872	Author, Caricaturist, Cartoonist
Maurice Ravel	Pisces	1875	Composer
Irwin Cobb	Gemini	1876	Humorist
Carl Sandburg	Capricorn	1878	Poet
Lionel Barrymore	Taurus	1878	Actor
James Branch Cabell	Aries	1879	Writer
Ethel Barrymore	Virgo	1879	Actress
Yoshihito Taisho Tenno	Leo	1879	Politician, Japanese ruler
E. M. Forster	Sagittarius	1879	Novelist
Rudolf Friml	Sagittarius	1879	Composer
Paul Klee	Sagittarius	1879	Artist, Painter
John Barrymore	Pisces	1882	Actor
Rockwell Kent	Cancer	1882	Artist, Author
Igor Stravinsky	Cancer	1882	Composer, Musicial innovator
Bela Lugosi	Scorpio	1882	Actor
Jean Giraudoux	Libra	1882	Author
Mack Sennett	Aquarius	1884	Producer, Director
Roy Chapman Andrews	Capricorn	1884	Explorer
Jean and Auguste Piccard	Capricorn	1884	Balloon pioneers
Harry Truman	Gemini	1884	Politician, President
W. A. Christiansen	Virgo	1885	Seeing-eye dogs, Blind worker
Wallace Beery	Aries	1886	Actor
Joyce Kilmer	Sagittarius	1886	Poet

NAME	MERCURY'S SIGN	YEAR	OCCUPATION
Diego Rivera	Sagittarius	1886	Artist, Painter
Rex Stout	Sagittarius	1886	Author, mysteries
Fatty Arbuckle	Pisces	1887	Actor, Comedian
Rupert Brooke	Leo	1887	Poet
Boris Karloff	Scorpio	1887	Actor
Roberto Assagioli	Pisces	1888	Psychologist
John Foster Dulles	Pisces	1888	Politician, Statesman
Barry Fitzgerald	Pisces	1888	Actor
Knute Rockne	Pisces	1888	Football coach
Richard Byrd	Scorpio	1888	Explorer, Adventurer
Sir George Wilkins	Scorpio	1888	Explorer of Australia
Erle Stanley Gardner	Cancer	1889	Author, mysteries
Aimee Semple McPherson	Libra	1889	Spiritual Evangelist
Sessue Hayakawa	Gemini	1890	Actor, Author
Hedda Hopper	Gemini	1890	Writer, Journalist
Vivian Robson	Gemini	1890	Astrologer
Roy de L. Munro	Libra	1890	Aviator
John McCormack	Capricorn	1891	Politician, Speaker of the House
Henry Miller	Capricorn	1891	Novelist
J. R. R. Tolkien	Capricorn	1892	Author, Linguist
Belle Bart	Virgo	1892	Astrologer
Prince Louis de Broglie	Virgo	1892	Physicist, Nobel Laureate, Author
Mae West	Virgo	1892	Actress

NAME	MERCURY'S SIGN	YEAR	OCCUPATION
Francesco Franco	Sagittarius	1892	Politician, Ruler of Spain
Jean Paul Getty	Sagittarius	1892	Industrialist, oil
Warner Baxter	Aries	1893	Actor
Harpo Marx	Sagittarius	1893	Actor, Comedian
Walter Brennan	Cancer	1894	Actor
Aldous Huxley	Cancer	1894	Author
Arthur Treacher	Cancer	1894	Actor
Jack Dempsey	Cancer	1895	Boxer
Juan Peron	Scorpio	1895	Politician
Lillian Gish	Libra	1896	Actress
Buster Keaton	Libra	1896	Actor, Comedian
William Faulkner	Virgo	1897	Novelist
Pope Paul VI	Virgo	1897	Pope
Paul Muni	Virgo or Libra	1897	Actor
Edgar Rice Burroughs	Virgo	1898	Author
Ngaio Marsh	Aries	1899	Author, mysteries
Vladimir Nabokov	Aries	1899	Novelist
Alfred Hitchcock	Virgo	1899	Producer, Director
Jorge Luis Borges	Leo	1899	Author
Charles Boyer	Leo	1899	Actor
James Wong Howe	Leo	1899	Cinematographer
Noel Coward	Sagittarius	1899	Playwright, Actor
Bruno Hauptmann	Sagittarius	1899	Convicted kidnapper, Murderer

NAME	MERCURY'S SIGN	YEAR	OCCUPATION
Erich Fromm	Aries	1900	Psychotherapist
Spencer Tracy	Pisces	1900	Actor
Elizabeth (Consort of George VI)	Leo	1900	Politician, Ruler
Aaron Copeland	Sagittarius	1900	Composer
Chester Gould	Scorpio	1900	Cartoonist
Manly Palmer Hall	Pisces	1901	Spiritual occultist
Andre Malraux	Scorpio	1901	Author, Philosopher, Warrior
Marian Anderson	Pisces	1902	Singer
John Steinbeck	Aquarius	1902	Novelist
Guy Lombardo	Cancer	1902	Musician, Bandleader
William Lear	Gemini	1902	Engineer
Henry Cabot Lodge II	Gemini	1902	Politician, Statesman
George Murphy	Gemini	1902	Actor, Politician
Richard Rodgers	Gemini	1902	Composer, Songwriter
William Wyler	Gemini	1902	Director
Elsa Lanchester	Libra	1902	Actress
Tallulah Bankhead	Aquarius	1903	Actress
Bob Hope	Gemini	1903	Actor, Comedian
Ray Bolger	Aquarius	1904	Actor
Marlene Dietrich	Capricorn	1904	Actress, Singer
Cary Grant	Capricorn	1904	Actor
Salvador Dali	Taurus	1904	Artist, Painter
Robert Montgomery	Taurus	1904	Actor

NAME	MERCURY'S SIGN	YEAR	OCCUPATION
Fats Waller	Taurus	1904	Singer, Songwriter, Pianist
Edmund Brown Sr.	Taurus	1905	Politician
James Mollison	Taurus	1905	Aviator
Robert Penn Warren	Taurus	1905	Author
Ernie Bushmiller	Virgo	1905	Cartoonist
Arthur Koestler	Virgo	1905	Author
Howard Hughes	Sagittarius	1905	Industrialist, Inventor, Aviator
Samuel Beckett	Aries	1906	Playwright
John Cameron Swayze	Aries	1906	Television broadcaster
John Huston	Leo	1906	Actor, Director
Agnes Morehead	Sagittarius	1906	Actress
Otto Preminger	Sagittarius	1906	Producer, Director
Ozzie Nelson	Pisces	1907	Actor, Bandleader, Musician
Jack Gilford	Leo	1907	Actor
Barbara Stanwyck	Leo	1907	Actress
Melvin Belli	Cancer	1907	Attorney
Francis Israel Regardie	Scorpio	1907	Occultist, Author, Psychotherapist
Rex Harrison	Pisces	1908	Actor
John Mills	Pisces	1908	Actor
Milton Berle	Cancer	1908	Actor, Comedian
Thurgood Marshall	Cancer	1908	Attorney, Supreme Court Justice
Nelson Rockefeller	Cancer	1908	Politician, Governor
Max Baer	Aquarius	1909	Boxer, Actor

NAME	MERCURY'S SIGN	YEAR	OCCUPATION
Dean Rusk	Aquarius	1909	Politician, Secretary of State
Errol Flynn	Gemini	1909	Actor
Burl Ives	Gemini	1909	Actor, Singer, Musician
Sam Yorty	Libra	1909	Politician
Django Reinhardt	Aquarius	1910	Musician, Songwriter, Guitarist
Scatman Crothers	Gemini	1910	Actor, Comedian
Richard English	Gemini	1910	Author
Artie Shaw	Gemini	1910	Bandleader, Musician
Rosalind Russell	Taurus	1910	Actress
Bonnie Parker	Virgo	1910	Outlaw
Betty Nuthall	Taurus	1911	Women's tennis pioneer
Julia Child	Virgo	1912	Author, Television personality, Chef
Ben Hogan	Virgo	1912	Golfer
Gene Kelly	Leo	1912	Actor, Dancer
Ted Key	Leo	1912	Cartoonist
Frankie Laine	Aries	1913	Singer
Karl Malden	Aries	1913	Actor
Sonja Henie	Pisces	1913	Skater
Hedy Lamarr	Scorpio	1914	Actress
Zero Mostel	Aquarius	1915	Actor
Fred Hoyle	Cancer	1915	Author
Arthur Miller	Scorpio	1915	Playwright
Victor Mature	Aquarius	1916	Actor

NAME	MERCURY'S SIGN	YEAR	OCCUPATION
Irwin Allen	Gemini	1916	Producer
Robert MacNamara	Gemini	1916	Politician
Portia Poder	Gemini	1916	Only known woman bullfighter
Trevor Howard	Libra	1916	Actor
Ernest Borgnine	Capricorn	1917	Actor
Yehudi Menuhin	Capricorn	1917	Musician, Violinist
Raymond Burr	Taurus	1917	Actor
Dennis Day	Taurus	1917	Actor, Singer
Norman Luboff	Taurus	1917	Conductor, Musician
Ella Fitzgerald	Taurus	1918	Singer
William Holden	Taurus	1918	Actor
Jack Paar	Taurus	1918	Television personality
Leonard Bernstein	Virgo	1918	Composer, Conductor, Musician
Ted Williams	Virgo	1918	Baseball player
Aleksandr Solzhenitzyn	Capricorn	1918	Author, Politician
Jose Greco	Sagittarius	1918	Dancer, Choreographer
Anwar Sadat	Sagittarius	1918	Politician
Helmut Schmidt	Sagittarius	1918	Politician
Howard Keel	Aries	1919	Actor
Madelyn Murray O'Hair	Aries	1919	Author, Atheist
Dino Delaurentis	Leo	1919	Producer
Rex Humbard	Leo	1919	Television evangelist
Hank Ketchum	Aries	1920	Cartoonist

NAME	MERCURY'S SIGN	YEAR	OCCUPATION
Leo McKern	Aries	1920	Actor
Marty Allen	Pisces	1920	Actor, Comedian
Howard Cosell	Pisces	1920	Television sportscaster
Werner Klemperer	Pisces	1920	Actor, Musician
George Shearing	Leo	1920	Composer, Musician
Isaac Stern	Leo	1920	Musician
Helen Thomas	Cancer	1920	Journalist, Dean of the White House Press Corps
Cord Meyer, Jr.	Scorpio or Sagittarius	1920	Reformer
Stan Musial	Scorpio	1920	Baseball player
Gene Tierney	Scorpio	1920	Actress
Cyd Charisse	Pisces	1921	Dancer
Betty Hutton	Pisces	1921	Actress
Gordon MacRae	Pisces	1921	Actor, Singer
Abe Vigoda	Pisces	1921	Actor
Nancy Reagan	Cancer	1921	Actress, Politician
Prince Phillip (Consort of Queen Elizabeth II)	Gemini or Cancer	1921	Politician, Ruler
Charles Bronson	Scorpio	1921	Actor
Bill Mauldin	Scorpio	1921	Political cartoonist
Patrick MacNee	Pisces	1922	Actor
John Anderson	Aquarius	1922	Politician
Helen Gurley Brown	Aquarius	1922	Author
Sybil Leek	Aquarius	1922	Occultist, Witch

NAME	MERCURY'S SIGN	YEAR	OCCUPATION
Leslie Nielsen	Aquarius	1922	Actor
Judy Garland	Cancer	1922	Actress, Singer
Rocky Graziano	Cancer	1922	Boxer
Eleanor Parker	Gemini	1922	Actress
Mo Udall	Gemini	1922	Politician
Jack Anderson	Libra	1922	Journalist, Investigative reporter
Carol Channing	Aquarius	1923	Actress, Singer
Norman Mailer	Aquarius	1923	Novelist, Journalist, Boxer, Playwright, Filmmaker
James Arness	Gemini	1923	Actor
Henry Kissinger	Gemini	1923	Politician, Secretary of State
Prince Ranier of Monaco	Gemini	1923	Politician, Ruler
Hank Williams	Libra	1923	Singer, Songwriter
Phillip Berrigan	Virgo	1923	Priest, Antiwar activist
Rod Serling	Capricorn	1924	Playwright, Television personality, Writer
Theodore Bikel	Taurus	1924	Actor, Singer
Lauren Bacall	Virgo	1924	Actress
Yvonne DeCarlo	Virgo	1924	Actress
Buddy Hackett	Virgo	1924	Actor, Comedian
Rocky Marciano	Virgo	1924	Boxer
Rod Steiger	Taurus	1925	Actor
Albert King	Aries	1925	Singer, Songwriter, Musician
Fess Parker	Virgo	1925	Actor

NAME	MERCURY'S SIGN	YEAR	OCCUPATION
Donald O'Connor	Leo	1925	Actor
Sammy Davis, Jr.	Sagittarius	1925	Singer, Dancer, Actor
Dick Van Dyke	Sagittarius	1925	Actor, Comedian, Singer
John Fowles	Aries	1926	Novelist
Virgil "Gus" Grissom	Aries	1926	Astronaut who died in a fire
Hugh Hefner	Aries	1926	Magazine editor, Publisher
Tony Bennett	Leo	1926	Singer
John Derek	Leo	1926	Actor, Director
Stan Freberg	Leo	1926	Writer, Comedian
Alice Ghostley	Leo	1926	Actress
Buddy Greco	Leo	1926	Singer
Leroy Gordon Cooper	Pisces	1927	Astronaut
Daniel Patrick Moynihan	Pisces	1927	Politician
George Plimpton	Pisces	1927	Author
Doc Severinsen	Leo	1927	Bandleader, Musician
John Chancellor	Cancer	1927	Television newscaster, Reporter
Patti Page	Scorpio	1927	Singer
Fats Domino	Pisces	1928	Singer, Songwriter, Musician
Larry Gelbart	Pisces	1928	Comedy writer, Producer
Vince Edwards	Cancer	1928	Actor
Gina Lollabrigida	Cancer	1928	Actress
Tony Franciosa	Libra	1928	Actor
Jules Lenier	Aquarius	1929	Stage magician

NAME	MERCURY'S SIGN	YEAR	OCCUPATION
Chuck Barris	Gemini	1929	Songwriter, Television producer
James McDivitt	Gemini	1929	Astronaut
Richard Gordon	Libra	1929	Astronaut
Edwin "Buzz" Aldrin	Aquarius	1930	Astronaut, Author
Gene Hackman	Capricorn	1930	Actor
Jack Lord	Capricorn	1930	Actor
Odetta	Capricorn	1930	Singer, Songwriter
Clint Eastwood	Taurus	1930	Actor, Producer, Director
Pernell Roberts	Taurus	1930	Actor
Ray Charles	Virgo	1930	Singer, Songwriter
Willie Mays	Taurus	1931	Baseball player
Joel Grey	Aries	1932	Actor, Dancer
Anthony Perkins	Aries	1932	Actor
Carl Perkins	Aries	1932	Singer, Songwriter, Musician
Debbie Reynolds	Aries	1932	Actress, Singer
Omar Sharif	Aries	1932	Actor
Mel Tillis	Virgo	1932	Singer, Songwriter, Musician
Mark Russell	Leo	1932	Political satirist
Melvin Van Peebles	Leo	1932	Actor, Director
Ellen Burstyn	Sagittarius	1932	Actress
Phillip Roth	Aries	1933	Novelist
Ed "Kookie" Byrnes	Leo	1933	Actor
Dom Deluise	Leo	1933	Actor, Comedian

NAME	MERCURY'S SIGN	YEAR	OCCUPATION
Robert Goulet	Scorpio	1933	Actor, Singer
Eugene Cernan	Pisces	1934	Astronaut
Sam Donaldson	Pisces	1934	Television newscaster, Reporter
Yuri Gagarin	Pisces	1934	Pioneer cosmonaut, Astronaut, First man in space
Ralph Nader	Pisces	1934	Author, Investigative reporter
Joyce Van Patten	Pisces	1934	Actress
Van Cliburn	Cancer	1934	Musician, Songwriter
Jean Marsh	Cancer	1934	Actress
Pat McCormick	Cancer	1934	Comedy writer
Donald Sutherland	Cancer	1934	Actor
Roger Chaffee	Aquarius	1935	Astronaut who died in a fire
Francoise Sagan	Gemini	1935	Playwright
Liuciano Pavarotti	Scorpio	1935	Opera singer
Alan Alda	Aquarius	1936	Actor, Screenwriter
Tammy Grimes	Aquarius	1936	Actress
James Darrin	Gemini	1936	Actor
Bruce Dern	Gemini	1936	Actor
Lou Gossett, Jr.	Gemini	1936	Actor
Tom T. Hall	Gemini	1936	Singer, Songwriter, Musician
Ruta Lee	Gemini	1936	Actress
Margaret O'Brien	Capricorn	1937	Actress
George Carlin	Taurus	1937	Writer, Comedian, Actor
Trini Lopez	Taurus	1937	Singer, Songwriter

NAME	MERCURY'S SIGN	YEAR	OCCUPATION
Brooks Robinson	Taurus	1937	Baseball player
Frankie Valli	Taurus	1937	Singer, Songwriter
Gus Trikonis	Capricorn	1938	Actor, Director
Glen Campbell	Taurus	1938	Singer, Songwriter, Musician
Rod McKuen	Aries	1938	Poet, Singer, Songwriter
Duane Eddy	Aries	1938	Musician, Songwriter
Elliott Gould	Virgo	1938	Actor
Diana Muldaur	Virgo	1938	Actress
Mason Williams	Virgo	1938	Musician, Composer, Author
Francis Ford Coppola	Aries	1939	Producer, Director
David Frost	Aries	1939	Television personality
Michael Learned	Aries	1939	Actress
Ali McGraw	Aries	1939	Actress
Cale Yarborough	Aries	1939	Race car driver
Peter Bogdanovich	Leo	1939	Director
George Hamilton	Leo	1939	Actor
Carole Shelley	Leo	1939	Actress
France Nuyen	Leo	1939	Actress
Luther Allison	Leo	1939	Blues guitarist
Lee Trevino	Sagittarius	1939	Golfer
Daniel Travanti	Aries	1940	Actor
Anita Bryant	Pisces	1940	Singer
James Caan	Pisces	1940	Actor
Joe Torre	Leo	1940	Baseball player

NAME	MERCURY'S SIGN	YEAR	OCCUPATION
Mary Jo Kopechne	Cancer	1940	Drowning victim
Terrance Stamp	Cancer	1940	Actor
Alex Trebec	Cancer	1940	Television personality
Buffy Ste. Marie	Pisces	1941	Singer, Songwriter, Musician
Helen Reddy	Scorpio	1941	Singer
Carole King	Aquarius	1942	Singer, Songwriter, Musician
Carol Lynley	Aquarius	1942	Actress
Graham Nash	Aquarius	1942	Singer, Songwriter, Musician
Bo Hopkins	Aquarius	1942	Actor
Roger Staubach	Aquarius	1942	Football player
Roger Ebert	Gemini	1942	Television critic
Curtis Mayfield	Gemini	1942	Singer, Songwriter, Musician
Paul McCartney	Gemini	1942	Singer, Songwriter, Musician, Screenwriter
Brian Wilson	Gemini	1942	Singer, Songwriter, Musician
Janis Joplin	Aquarius	1943	Singer, Songwriter, Musician
Katharine Ross	Capricorn	1943	Actress
Gary Burghoff	Gemini	1943	Actor
Jessi Colter	Gemini	1943	Singer, Songwriter, Musician
Leslie Uggams	Gemini	1943	Actress, Singer
Joe Namath	Taurus	1943	Football player
Joe Frazier	Capricorn	1944	Boxer
Marjoe Gortner	Capricorn	1944	Boy evangelist, Actor, Producer
Michael Tilson Thomas	Capricorn	1944	Conductor

NAME	MERCURY'S SIGN	YEAR	OCCUPATION
Jill Clayburgh	Taurus	1944	Actress
Steve Martin	Virgo	1945	Actor, Comedian
Ken Norton	Virgo	1945	Boxer
Nona Hendryx	Leo	1945	Singer
Linda Kelsey	Leo	1946	Actress
Ry Cooder	Pisces	1947	Singer, Songwriter, Musician
Billy Crystal	Pisces	1947	Actor, Comedian
Albert Brooks	Cancer	1947	Actor, Producer, Director
Betty Buckley	Cancer	1947	Actress
Arlo Guthrie	Cancer	1947	Singer, Songwriter, Musician
O. J. Simpson	Cancer	1947	Football player
Cat Stevens	Cancer	1947	Singer, Songwriter, Musician
Bernadette Peters	Aquarius	1948	Actress
Todd Rundgren	Cancer	1948	Singer, Songwriter, Musician
Clarence Thomas	Cancer	1948	Attorney, Supreme Court Justice
Natalie Cole	Aquarius	1949	Singer
Brooke Adams	Aquarius	1949	Actress
Hank Williams, Jr.	Gemini	1949	Singer, Songwriter, Musician
Stevie Wonder	Taurus	1950	Singer, Songwriter, Musician
Marilou Henner	Aries	1952	Actress
Pat McDonald	Leo	1952	Singer, Songwriter
Reginald Veljohnson	Leo	1952	Actor
Johnathan Frakes	Leo	1952	Actor

NAME	MERCURY'S SIGN	YEAR	OCCUPATION
Robert Cray	Cancer	1953	Blues guitarist
Louise Mandrell	Cancer	1954	Singer, Songwriter, Musician
John Grisham	Aquarius	1955	Author
Griffin Dunne	Gemini	1955	Actor
Andrew Stevens	Gemini	1955	Actor
Sugar Ray Leonard	Gemini	1956	Boxer
Belinda Carlisle	Virgo	1958	Singer
Madonna Ciccone	Virgo	1958	Singer, Songwriter, Actress, Author
Angela Bassett	Virgo	1958	Actress
Madeleine Stowe	Virgo	1958	Actress
Steve Guttenberg	Leo	1958	Actor
Victoria Jackson	Leo	1959	Actress
Rosanna Arquette	Leo	1959	Actress
Ivan Lendl	Pisces	1960	Tennis player
Christopher Adkins	Pisces	1961	Actor
Wynton Marsalis	Scorpio	1961	Musician, Songwriter
Garth Brooks	Aquarius	1962	Singer, Musician
Clint Black	Aquarius	1962	Singer, Musician
Ally Sheedy	Gemini	1962	Actress
Melissa Gilbert	Taurus	1964	Actress
Mats Wilander	Virgo	1964	Tennis player
Steve Gorman	Leo	1965	Musician
Kyra Sedgwick	Leo	1965	Actress

NAME	MERCURY'S SIGN	YEAR	OCCUPATION
Kevin Dillon	Leo	1965	Actor
Gary Coleman	Pisces	1968	Actor
Molly Ringwald	Aquarius	1968	Actress
Mary Joe Fernandez	Virgo	1971	Tennis player

Famous People Born with Mercury Stationary or Stationary Direct

NAME	MERCURY'S SIGN	YEAR	OCCUPATION
Vincent Van Gogh	SR Aries	1853	Painter
John Phillip Sousa	SR Sagittarius	1854	Composer
Ignace Paderewski	SR Sagittarius	1860	Composer, Musician, Statesman
John Galsworthy	SD Leo	1867	Novelist
George Russell (A. E.)	SD Pisces	1867	Poet, Mystic
William S. Hart	SR Sagittarius	1870	Actor
Sri Aurobindo	SR Virgo	1872	Poet, Mystic, Author
Pancho Villa	SD Virgo	1877	Revolutionary
Upton Sinclair	SD Virgo	1878	Novelist
Joseph Stalin	SD Sagittarius	1879	Outlaw, Politician, Dictator
Hermann Keyserling	SR Leo	1880	Philosopher
Eduard Benes	SD Taurus	1884	Statesman
Isak Dinesen	SR Taurus	1885	Author
D. H. Lawrence	SD Virgo	1885	Novelist, Poet
Boris Pasternak	SD Aquarius	1890	Author
Eddie Rickenbacker	SD Libra	1890	Aviator, Race car driver
Mary Pickford	SR Taurus	1892	Actress
Manfred Von Richthofen	SD Aries	1892	Aviator, "The Red Baron"
Buckminister Fuller	SD Cancer	1895	Philosopher
Oscar Hammerstein	SD Cancer	1895	Composer
F. Scott Fitzgerald	SR Libra	1896	Novelist
Jimmie Rodgers	SR Libra	1897	Singer, Songwriter
Noel Coward	SD Sagittarius	1899	Dramatist, Playwright

NAME	MERCURY'S SIGN	YEAR	OCCUPATION
Bruno Hauptman	SR Sagittarius	1899	Convicted kidnapper
Norma Shearer	SD Leo	1900	Actress
Linus Pauling	SR Pisces	1901	Scientist, Nobel Laureate
Randolph Scott	SR Aquarius	1903	Actor
Louis Dewohl	SR Aquarius	1903	Astrologer
Bing Crosby	SR Taurus	1904	Singer, Actor, Producer
Howard Hughes	SD Sagittarius	1905	Aviator, Inventor
Little Brother Montgomery	SD Aries	1906	Blues pianist
Leo Durocher	SR Leo	1906	Baseball player, Manager
Thelma Todd	SR Leo	1906	Actress, Comedienne
Len Harvey	SR Leo	1907	Boxer
John Kenneth Galbraith	SR Scorpio	1908	Economist
Eric Ambler	SD Gemini	1909	Suspense novelist
Al Capp	SD Libra	1909	Cartoonist (L'il Abner)
Constance Cummings	SR Gemini	1910	Actress
Maureen O'Sullivan	SD Taurus	1911	Actress
William Golding	SD Virgo	1911	Novelist
Kenneth Patchen	SR Capricorn	1911	Author, Poet
Mary Martin	SD Scorpio	1913	Actress
Jonas Salk	SR Scorpio	1914	Medical researcher, Discovered polio vaccine
Dylan Thomas	SR Scorpio	1914	Writer, Poet
Lorne Green	SR Pisces	1915	Actor

NAME	MERCURY'S SIGN	YEAR	OCCUPATION
David Rockefeller	SR Cancer	1915	Banker, Trilateralist
John F. Kennedy	SD Taurus	1917	Politician, President
Henry Ford II	SR Libra	1917	Auto manufacturer
Mike Wallace	SD Taurus	1918	Television journalist
Spike Milligan	SR Taurus	1918	Actor, Comedian, Musician
George Wallace	SD Leo	1919	Politician
Curt Gowdy	SR Leo	1919	Television sportscaster
Jack Webb	SD Pisces	1920	Actor, Producer
Toshire Mifune	SD Pisces	1920	Actor
Yul Brynner	SD Leo	1920	Actor
Ricardo Montalban	SD Scorpio	1920	Actor
John Glenn	SD Cancer	1921	Astronaut, Politician
Joseph Papp	SR Cancer	1921	Broadway Producer
Gower Champion	SR Cancer	1921	Choreographer, Dancer
Jacqueline Nourrit	SR Cancer	1921	Musical prodigy
Jean Stapleton	SR Aquarius	1923	Actress
Kathryn Grayson	SD Capricorn	1923	Actress
Peggy Cass	SD Taurus	1924	Actress
Scott Carpenter	SD Aries	1925	Astronaut
Ross McWhirter	SR Virgo	1925	Author, Founded *Guiness Book of World Records* with brother Norris
Harry Belafonte	SR Pisces	1927	Singer, Actor, Humanitarian
Anthony Lewis	SD Pisces	1927	Newspaper columnist

NAME	MERCURY'S SIGN	YEAR	OCCUPATION
Neil Simon	SR Leo	1927	Playwright
Janet Leigh	SR Leo	1927	Actress
Amanda Blake	SD Aquarius	1929	Actress
Francoise Gauquelin	SD Gemini	1929	Scientific researcher, Author
Rod Taylor	SR Aquarius	1930	Actor
James Earl Jones	SD Capricorn	1931	Actor
Meadowlark Lemon	SD Aries	1932	Basketball player
Peter O'Toole	SR Virgo	1932	Actor
Abbie Lane	SD Sagittarius	1932	Singer
Wayne Rogers	SD Pisces	1933	Actor
Michael Caine	SR Aries	1933	Actor
Quincy Jones	SR Aries	1933	Musician, Arranger, Humanitarian
Julian Bream	SR Leo	1933	Classical guitarist
Jerry Falwell	SD Leo	1933	Evangelist, Politician
John Mayall	SD Scorpio	1933	Blues musician, Singer
Anna Moffo	SR Cancer	1934	Opera singer
Burt Reynolds	SD Aquarius	1936	Actor
Joe Don Baker	SD Aquarius	1936	Actor
Bobby Darin	SD Gemini	1936	Singer
Steven Breyer	SR Virgo	1938	Attorney, Supreme Court Justice
Kenny Rogers	SR Virgo	1938	Singer, Actor
Claudia Cardinale	SD Aries	1939	Actress

NAME	MERCURY'S SIGN	YEAR	OCCUPATION
Dusty Springfield	SD Aries	1939	Singer
Clarence Williams III	SD Leo	1939	Actor
Brooks Robinson	SD Leo	1939	Baseball player
Ginger Baker	SD Leo	1939	Drummer
Carl Yastrzemski	SD Leo	1939	Baseball player
Ringo Starr	SR Leo	1940	Musician, Actor
Martin Sheen	SD Cancer	1940	Actor, Activist
Barbara Feldon	SD Aquarius	1941	Actress
Paul Simon	SR Scorpio	1941	Singer, Composer
Art Garfunkel	SD Libra	1941	Singer, Composer
Michelle Lee	SD Gemini	1942	Actress
Fabian Forte	SD Capricorn	1943	Singer
Gayle Hunnicutt	SD Capricorn	1943	Actress
John Denver	SR Capricorn	1943	Singer, Songwriter, Actor
Shelly Fabares	SD Capricorn	1944	Singer, Actress
George Lucas	SD Taurus	1944	Film innovator, Producer, Director
Jim Capaldi	SR Virgo	1944	Musician
Antonia Novello	SR Virgo	1944	Surgeon General
Catherine Spaak	SR Aries	1945	Actress
Loni Anderson	SR Virgo	1945	Actress
Susan St. James	SD Leo	1946	Actress
Kim Carnes	SR Leo	1946	Singer
Twiggy	SR Libra	1949	Model, Actress

NAME	MERCURY'S SIGN	YEAR	OCCUPATION
Barbi Benton	SD Capricorn	1950	Actress, Singer
Joe Strummer	SD Leo	1952	Musician
John Travolta	SR Pisces	1954	Actor
Patty Hearst	SR Pisces	1954	Outlaw
Bjorn Borg	SD Gemini	1956	Tennis player
Ervin "Magic" Johnson	SD Leo	1959	Basketball player
Danny Bonaduce	SD Leo	1959	Actor
Boy George	SR Cancer	1961	Singer
Marlee Matlin	SD Leo	1965	Actress
Jonathan Silverman	SD Leo	1966	Actor
Pete Sampras	SR Virgo	1971	Tennis player
Tempestt Bledsoe	SD Cancer	1973	Actress

8

FAMOUS OCCURRENCES DURING MERCURY RETROGRADE

DURING A MERCURY RETROGRADE period, I started to wonder if there was a consistent pattern of events that occur during Mercury retrograde periods. I discovered some historic Mercury retrograde events that intrigued me, such as women receiving the right to vote in Utah territory during a Mercury retrograde in 1870, or the great Jonas Salk announcing his breakthrough polio vaccine in 1953. Well-known fugitives are often caught during a Mercury retrograde.

Other occurrences disturbed me for a Mercury retrograde indicates something seemingly unresolvable, or destined to reappear, again and again through history. This seemed to apply to events such as the outlawing of slavery in this country, the liberation of Buchenwald, Three Mile Island and the Camp David accords, as well as oil spills and nuclear tests too numerous to mention. It is truly a shame that the core issues these events represent were not resolved conclusively when they occurred, and that we may be forced to reexamine these issues time and time again.

Of course, that these events occurred during Mercury retrograde may indicate that they are collective issues of long standing, and that they need a constant and regular review. Perhaps the social-spiritual dimension of Mercury retrograde makes it necessary for us to have a constant and ongoing public and open dialogue about our collective shadows. There are important things that come up, in the "real world" as well as philosophically and spiritually, during Mercury retrograde periods. These periods may be the times that nature has built into the larger plan so we can take a new look at how we are (or are not) dealing with larger, but important, issues and assumptions. This evolution through reflection after the fact seems to be an important part of our collective process of coming out of the darkness into the light.

The following list is, of course, incomplete, but any thorough list would run hundreds of pages. Here I have simply listed the event, what year it happened, and the sign in which Mercury was retrograde. If an event occurred within a day of when Mercury was stationary direct or stationary retrograde, these are indicated by an (SD) or an (SR). When the event occurred on the cusp, both signs are listed.

I have mainly limited this list to events since 1850, though a few interesting ones have been included from prior eras. As you explore the many patterns in this list of significant events from the last century-and-a-half of world history, you will see that anything can happen during Mercury retrograde!

The facts and dates were compiled from a variety of sources including:

Associated Press, "Today In History" (New York: Associated Press, daily);

Front page: 100 years of the Los Angeles Times, 1881–1981: Introduction, Otis Chandler, publisher's note, W. Thomas Johnson; editor's note, William F. Thomas, text by Digby Diehl (New York: H. N. Abrams, 1981);

Page one: Major Events 1920–1994, as presented in the New York Times (New York: Galahad books, 1994);

New York Times (New York: The New York Times, daily);

Facts on File (New York: Facts on File, weekly);

Leonard, Thomas M., *Day by Day: The Forties* (New York: Facts on Files, c1977);

Merritt, Jeffrey D., *Day by Day: The Fifties* (New York: Facts on Files, 1979);

Parker, Thomas, and Douglas Nelson, *Day by Day: The Sixties* (New York: Facts on Files, c1983);
Leonard, Thomas, Cynthia Crippen, and Marc Aronson, *Day by Day: The Seventies* (New York: Facts on File, c1988);
Meltzer, Ellen, and Marc Aronson, *Day by Day: The Eighties* (New York: Facts on File, c1995).

MERCURY RETROGRADE EVENTS

☿℞ Macbeth, King of Scotland, was slain by the son of King Duncan, 1057; Leo.

☿℞ Joan of Arc captured by Burgundians and sold to British, 1430; Taurus (SD).

☿℞ Columbus set sail from Spain on the voyage that would take him to the Americas for the first time, 1492; Leo (SD).

☿℞ Columbus left Cadiz on his fourth and final trip to Western hemisphere, 1502; Gemini.

☿℞ England's King Henry VIII died; succeeded by his 9 year old son, Edward VI, 1547; Aquarius.

☿℞ Mary, Queen of Scots, beheaded by England's Queen Elizabeth I, 1587; Aquarius.

☿℞ Spanish Armada set sail to invade England; after unexpected storms, it was destroyed by England in August, 1588; Taurus.

☿℞ Galileo Galilei arrived in Rome for trial before the Inquisition, 1633; Aquarius.

☿℞ Peter Stuyvesant arrived in New Amsterdam to become governor, 1647; Gemini (SR).

☿℞ New Amsterdam (now New York City) incorporated, 1653, Aquarius.

☿℞ Jury acquitted John Peter Zenger of the *New York Weekly Journal* on charges of seditious libel, 1735; Leo.

☿℞ Patrick Henry of Virginia denounced the Stamp Act and when accused of treason, he stated "If this be treason, make the most of it!", 1765; Gemini.

☿℞ US colonies won official recognition from France, 1778; Aquarius.

☿ℝ Constitutional Convention began to debate a draft of the US Constitution in Philadelphia, 1787; Virgo (SR).

☿ℝ NY Stock Exchange founded under a tree on what is now Wall St., 1792; Taurus.

☿ℝ Robert Fulton's steamboat, "The Clermont," began its first round trip up the Hudson River to Albany, 1807; Leo.

☿ℝ Paul Revere died, 1818; Gemini (SR).

☿ℝ Michigan became 26th state, 1837; Aquarius (SR).

☿ℝ For the only time in history, the US Senate selected the VP of the US after no candidate received a majority of the electoral vote, 1837; Aquarius.

☿ℝ Samuel F. B. Morse opened America's first telegraph line, 1844; Gemini.

☿ℝ American flag raised for the first time over Los Angeles, 1846; Virgo (SR).

☿ℝ US Army captured Santa Fe and annexed all of New Mexico, 1846; Virgo.

☿ℝ Maine became the first state to prohibit alcohol, 1851; Taurus (SD).

☿ℝ Thoreau published *Walden*, describing his experiences at Walden Pond, 1854; Leo.

☿ℝ Minnesota became a state, 1858; Taurus.

☿ℝ Ground broken for Suez Canal, 1859; Aries.

☿ℝ Corkscrew patented in NYC, 1860; Aries.

☿ℝ Pony Express started first run, 1860; Aries.

☿ℝ US government levied an income tax for the first time, 1861; Cancer (SD).

☿ℝ Congress authorized Medal of Honor, 1862; Cancer.

☿ℝ Slavery outlawed in US, 1862; Cancer.

☿ℝ West Virginia became a state, 1863; Gemini.

☿ℝ John Wilkes Booth caught; Jefferson Davis caught, 1865; Taurus.

☿ℝ Seward reached agreement with Russia to buy Alaska, 1867; Aries.

☿ℝ President Andrew Johnson suspended Secretary of War Stanton; sparked first impeachment proceeding against a US President in history, 1867; Leo (SD).

☿℞ Virginia rejoined the Union, 1870; Aquarius.

☿℞ US Weather Bureau established, 1870; Aquarius.

☿℞ "The Cardiff Giant," supposedly petrified human remains, were revealed to be carved gypsum, 1870; Aquarius.

☿℞ Women in the Utah Territory gained the right to vote, 1870; Aquarius.

☿℞ The National League of Professional Base Ball Clubs formed in NY, 1876; Pisces (SR).

☿℞ Custer massacred at Little Big Horn, 1876; Gemini.

☿℞ Sitting Bull surrendered, 1881; Cancer.

☿℞ Billy the Kid shot, 1881; Cancer.

☿℞ A rumor the Brooklyn Bridge was going to collapse caused a stampede, killing 12 people, 1883; Gemini.

☿℞ Helen Keller was taught her first word ("water"), 1887; Pisces.

☿℞ North and South Dakota, Montana, and Washington state admitted to US, 1889; Aquarius.

☿℞ Carnegie (Music) Hall opened in NYC, 1891; Taurus.

☿℞ Spanish American War started, 1898; Aries.

☿℞ International forces entered Beijing to quash Boxer Rebellion, 1900; Leo (SD).

☿℞ Henry Ford incorporated Ford Motor Company, 1903; Gemini.

☿℞ First Olympic games held in US opened in St. Louis, 1904; Taurus.

☿℞ San Francisco earthquake, 1906; Aries (SD).

☿℞ William H. Taft elected US President, 1908; Libra.

☿℞ NAACP, America's oldest civil rights organization, founded, 1909; Aquarius.

☿℞ Boy Scouts of America incorporated, 1910; Capricorn (SD).

☿℞ Halley's Comet moved across the Sun, 1910; Gemini.

☿℞ Union of South Africa formed, 1910; Gemini.

☿℞ Supreme Court ordered Standard Oil breakup, 1911; Taurus.

☿℞ Roald Amundsen discovered South Pole, 1911; Capricorn (SR).

☿℞ The Titanic sank off the coast of Newfoundland, 1912; Aries.

☿℞ President Wilson appointed Louis Brandeis to Supreme Court, becoming its first Jewish member, 1916; Aquarius (SR).

☿℞ Vision of the Virgin Mary at Fatima, Portugal, 1917; Taurus.

☿℞ Warren G. Harding wins US Presidency, 1920; Sagittarius.

☿℞ Anti-Japanese land law passed in US, 1920; Sagittarius.

☿℞ President Harding signed bill ending WW I, 1921; Cancer.

☿℞ Truce in Ireland declared, 1921; Cancer.

☿℞ Republicans proposed first ever federal sales tax, 1922; Aquarius.

☿℞ Lenin died of cerebral hemorrhage, 1924; Capricorn.

☿℞ "Experts" proposed independent gold bank under international control, 1924, Capricorn (SD).

☿℞ J. Edgar Hoover given post as FBI Director, 1924; Taurus.

☿℞ Warner Brothers premiered Vitaphone sound-on-disc movie system, 1926; Leo.

☿℞ Gertrude Ederle became first woman to swim the English Channel, 1926; Leo.

☿℞ Amelia Earhart flew the Atlantic Ocean, 1928; Cancer (SR).

☿℞ Italy recognized Vatican City's independence and sovereignty, 1929; Aquarius.

☿℞ First airline stewardess went on duty, 1930; Gemini.

☿℞ Empire State Building dedicated, 1931; Taurus.

☿℞ Mafia Crime Commission formed, 1931; Virgo (SD).

☿℞ Amelia Earhart became the first woman to fly non-stop across US, 1932; Leo (SD).

☿℞ Wiley Post completed first around-the-world solo flight, 1933; Leo.

☿℞ Hitler violently purged Nazi party, 1934; Cancer (SR).

☿℞ John Dillinger shot, 1934; Cancer (SD).

☿℞ Bruno Hauptman falsely convicted for Lindbergh kidnapping, 1935; Pisces.

☿℞ Alcoholics Anonymous founded, 1935; Cancer (SR).

☿℞ First members of baseball's Hall of Fame named, 1936; Aquarius.

☿℞ Margaret Mitchell won the Pulitzer Prize for *Gone with the Wind*, 1937; Taurus.

☿℞ Dirigible Hindenburg exploded at Lakehurst N.A.S., 1937; Taurus.

☿℞ George VI crowned King of Great Britain, 1937; Taurus.

☿℞ Eleanor Roosevelt proposed a salary and 8 hour workdays for mothers, 1937; Taurus.

☿℞ Marian Anderson sang at the Lincoln Memorial, 1939; Aries.

☿℞ Albert Einstein signed a letter to FDR urging creation of an atomic weapons research program, 1939; Leo.

☿℞ Russians invaded Finland, 1939; Sagittarius.

☿℞ International Labor Organization postponed annual meeting for a year, 1940; Pisces.

☿℞ All-India National Congress voted to pursue independence from Britain, 1940; Pisces.

☿℞ Gallup Poll said 53 percent of US voters would not support FDR for a third term, 1940; Pisces.

☿℞ All-India Congress demanded total independence from Great Britain, 1940; Leo (SR).

☿℞ Nazis confiscated French art treasures, 1940; Leo.

☿℞ Hitler ordered preparation for British invasion; Battle of Britain began, 1940; Leo.

☿℞ Trans-Pacific mail service inaugurated, 1940; Leo.

☿℞ American Football League formed with six teams, 1940; Leo.

☿℞ First peacetime draft lottery in US history, 1940; Scorpio (SR).

☿℞ Sulfa announced as a cure for dysentery, 1940; Scorpio.

☿℞ Worst earthquake in Rumanian history killed 1000, 1940; Scorpio.

☿℞ FDR re-elected to become the first third-term president in history, 1940; Scorpio.

☿℞ Tacoma Narrows bridge, completed the previous July, fell 190 feet into Puget Sound injuring no one, 1940; Scorpio.

☿℞ "Fantasia" opened in NYC with Leopold Stokowski conducting the score, 1940; Scorpio.

☿℞ Lend-Lease approved, 1941; Aquarius.

☿℞ Delaware State Assembly repealed 200-year-old Sunday "Blue Laws," 1941; Aquarius.

☿℞ USSR archeologists opened the tomb of Tamerlane, 14th century Mongol warrior, in Samarkand, 1941; Cancer (SR).

☿℞ Hitler began war on Russia, 1941; Cancer (SR).

☿℞ Pope Pius XII declared that "black paganism" was sweeping the world, 1941; Cancer.

☿℞ Clash between Swiss-German nudists and Panamanian police killed ten and wounded eight, 1941; Cancer.

☿℞ US Army admitted building a concentration camp on Long Island, 1941; Scorpio.

☿℞ Vatican newspaper urged Italians not to read most novels "because they are immoral and lead to sensuality and decadence," 1941; Scorpio.

☿℞ FDR signed six billion dollar Lend-Lease bill, 1941; Scorpio.

☿℞ Secret Japanese Cabinet meeting decided for war with US, 1941; Libra.

☿℞ Former US ambassador to USSR stated Stalin purges of 1935–1938 were mainly of those in the employ of the Japanese and German High Commands, 1941; Libra.

☿℞ Brazil prohibited speaking Japanese, German, or Italian in public, 1942; Aquarius (SR).

☿℞ Ethiopia abolished slavery, 1942; Aquarius.

☿℞ Dies Committee in US government recommended all Japanese on the west coast of the US be removed at least 500 miles inland, 1942; Aquarius.

☿℞ War Time adopted in the US, 1942; Aquarius.

☿℞ Jinnah proposed post-war partition of India, 1942; Aquarius (SD).

☿℞ Mexico declared war against Germany, Italy, and Japan May 30, and then agreed that war had already existed since May 22, 1942; Gemini (SR).

☿℞ Alien property custodian Crowley seized 600 "enemy-owned" patents in science and aviation, 1942; Gemini.

☿℞ Wartime Civil Control Administration announced all west coast Japanese had been removed inland, 1942; Gemini.

☿℞ Armour Research Foundation announced patent on portable recording device, 1942; Gemini.

☿℞ Battle of Midway, the turning point of the Pacific War, 1942; Gemini.

☿℞ Japanese shelled Vancouver, 1942; Gemini.

☿℞ Japanese invaded Aleutian Islands June 3; reached farthest point east June 22, 1942; Gemini (SD).

☿℞ Eleanor Roosevelt advocated voting rights for ages 18 and up, 1943; Aquarius.

☿℞ Senator Gillette proposed ERA amendment, 1943; Aquarius.

☿℞ Russians claimed victory at Stalingrad, 1943; Capricorn.

☿℞ Tennessee voted to repeal 50-year-old poll tax, 1943; Capricorn.

☿℞ US Army began to accept enlistments from American-born Japanese, 1943; Capricorn.

☿℞ Battle of Guadalcanal ended, 1943; Capricorn (SD).

☿℞ Fire destroyed the National Library of Peru (100,000 rare volumes, 40,000 manuscripts), 1943; Gemini (SR).

☿℞ Axis forces in N. Africa surrendered, 1943; Gemini (SR).

☿℞ 70,000 Jews killed or sent to camps in Warsaw Ghetto, 1943; Gemini.

☿℞ Norman Rockwell's "Rosie the Riveter" appeared on the cover of the *Saturday Evening Post*, 1943; Taurus.

☿℞ Leslie Howard shot down over English Channel, 1943; Taurus.

☿℞ Sweden announced it will give asylum to 7000 Jews arrested in Denmark two days earlier, 1943; Virgo.

☿℞ "All political activity" outlawed in Argentina, 1944; Capricorn.

☿℞ Mexico issued a decree ending the siesta, 1944; Taurus.

☿℞ First eyebank in US established in NYC, 1944; Taurus.

☿℞ Nazis surrender Paris, 1944; Virgo (SR).

☿℞ Harvard announced synthetic skin, 1944; Virgo.

☿℞ Battle of the Bulge began at Bastogne, Belgium, 1944; Capricorn (SR).

☿℞ Supreme Court upheld constitutionality of Japanese internment laws, 1944; Capricorn.

☿℞ US troops discovered Nazi hoard of gold, currency, and art in salt mine, 1945; Aries.

☿℞ US Senate ratified water pact with Mexico "guaranteeing" them 1.5 million acre-feet of water annually from the Colorado River, 1945; Aries.

☿℞ General George Patton liberated Buchenwald, 1945; Aries.

☿℞ Atomic bombs dropped on Hiroshima and Nagasaki, Russia declared war on Japan, Japan surrendered, 1945; Virgo (SR).

☿℞ Georgia adopted first new constitution since 1877, 1945; Virgo (SR).

☿℞ Truman signed UN charter, making the US the first nation to do so, 1945; Virgo (SR).

☿℞ USSR and China signed a "treaty of friendship and alliance," 1945; Virgo.

☿℞ UN Preparatory Commission voted to establish UN HQ in US, 1945; Sagittarius (SR).

☿℞ Newfoundland regained the right of self-rule lost in 1933, 1945; Sagittarius.

☿℞ Cholera, bubonic plague, small pox, meningitis epidemics in China, 1946; Aries.

☿℞ United Nations set up temporary headquarters at Hunter College, NYC, 1946; Aries.

☿℞ ERA failed in the US Senate, 1946; Leo (SR).

☿℞ 60 nations signed World Health Organization charter, 1946; Leo (SR).

☿℞ First underwater atomic test at Bikini Atoll, 1946; Leo.

☿℞ Atomic Energy Commission established, 1946; Leo.

☿℞ President Truman signed Fulbright Scholarship Program into law, 1946; Leo.

☿℞ Bermuda dropped its 38-year ban on private autos, 1946; Leo.

☿℞ First sale of radioactive isotopes to a private institute (a hospital), 1946; Leo.

☿℞ Vietnam approved democratic constitution, 1946; Sagittarius (SR).

☿℞ Previously unknown manuscript by Benjamin Franklin for a string quartet found in Paris, 1946; Sagittarius.

☿℞ Black and white Baptists met for the first time in history in Georgia, 1946; Sagittarius.

☿℞ Supreme Court upheld Tillamook Indian claim for payment for land taken from them, 1946; Scorpio.

☿℞ Dumont labs demonstrated picture and sound transmission by light, 1946; Scorpio.

☿℞ International Monetary Fund began operations, 1947; Pisces (SR).

☿℞ India abolished salt tax and doubled corporate tax, 1947; Pisces (SR).

☿℞ US and Philippines signed 99-year treaty guaranteeing US bases there, 1947; Pisces.

☿℞ FCC ruled against commercial use of CBS color TV system, ruling for black and white, 1947; Pisces.

☿℞ US government approved Hawaiian statehood bill, 1947; Pisces.

☿℞ US Air Force introduced daily weather flights over North Pole, 1947; Pisces (SD).

☿℞ Pan Am completed first globe circling commercial flight, 1947; Cancer (SR).

☿℞ Mississippi River reached highest crest in 104 years, 1947; Cancer (SR).

☿℞ Bill for equal pay for male and female factory workers introduced, 1947; Cancer.

☿℞ Work began on future UN site in NYC, 1947; Cancer.

☿℞ US House of Representatives voted for loyalty investigation of federal employees, 1947; Cancer.

☿℞ Truman signed bill changing the line of presidential succession, 1947; Cancer.

☿℞ Atomic Energy Commission revealed plans to Congress for Pacific Ocean nuclear proving ground, 1947; Cancer.

☿℞ Presidential Civil Rights Committee submitted 178-page report suggesting pioneering civil rights recommendations, 1947; Scorpio.

☿℞ India invaded Kashmir, 1947; Scorpio.

☿℞ British government announced first potato rationing since WW I, 1947; Scorpio.

☿℞ New Orleans federal court ruled equally qualified black and white teachers must receive the same pay, 1947; Scorpio.

☿℞ Nancy Leftenant was the first black admitted to the Army Nurse Corps, 1948; Pisces (SR).

☿℞ First successful scaling of Mt. Aconcagua, highest peak in Western hemisphere, 1948; Pisces (SR).

☿℞ "Kitty Hawk" airplane returned to US from London announced, 1948; Pisces.

☿℞ Chuck Yeager broke the sound barrier for the first time, 1948; Cancer (SR).

☿℞ UN began negotiations for permanent peace settlement in Palestine, 1948; Cancer.

☿℞ Berlin blockade began, 1948; Cancer.

☿℞ First televised US political party convention, 1948; Cancer.

☿℞ The last exhibition flight of the US military's last fighter biplane, 1948; Scorpio.

☿℞ *NY Times* survey asserted 333 electoral votes for Dewey, 82 for Truman, 1948; Libra.

☿℞ NYC began fluoridation program for children, 1948; Libra.

☿℞ Xerography inkless reproduction process publicly demonstrated for the first time, 1948; Libra.

☿℞ Ultrafax radio device for transmitting pictures demonstrated for the first time, 1948; Libra.

☿℞ Senate issued report stating that twenty big oil companies dominate the industry, and oil shortages of 1948 were induced to increase profits, 1949; Aquarius.

☿℞ The first daytime TV soap opera broadcast, 1949; Aquarius.

☿℞ 20 people died in a riot in Ecuador following a radio broadcast of "War of the Worlds," 1949; Aquarius.

☿℞ AMA favored national health care proposal over medical insurance plan, 1949; Aquarius (SD).

☿℞ Kansas ended 69-year ban on alcohol, 1949; Gemini.

☿℞ Prominent entertainers accused of being Communists: Frank Sinatra, Orson Welles, Pearl Buck, Dashiell Hammett, Thomas Mann, others, 1949; Gemini.

☿℞ *1984* published in NY, 1949; Gemini.

☿℞ University of California, Berkeley, required loyalty oath of faculty, 1949; Gemini.

☿℞ Soviets exploded nuclear device for first time, 1949; Libra (SR).

☿℞ Mao Tse-Tung proclaimed the People's Republic of China, 1949; Libra (SR).

☿℞ Berlin airlift ended, 1949; Libra.

☿℞ Yugoslavia severed ties with USSR, 1949; Libra.

☿℞ 10,000 striking Italian workers clashed with police; five deaths lead to a strike by one million workers the next day, 1950; Aquarius (SR).

☿℞ USSR revived death penalty abolished three years earlier, 1950; Aquarius.

☿℞ UN studied wiretap charges against J. Edgar Hoover, 1950; Aquarius.

☿℞ US Senate introduced a bill to extend the peacetime draft $3\frac{1}{2}$ years, 1950; Aquarius.

☿℞ Rutgers directed all campus organizations to abolish race and religion restrictions, 1950; Capricorn.

☿℞ New minimum wage law went into effect, rose from 40 to 75 cents an hour, 1950; Capricorn.

☿℞ India officially became a republic, with Nehru as Premier, 1950; Capricorn.

☿℞ La Jolla remains indicated N. American human life 40,000 years ago, tripled previous estimate, 1950; Capricorn (SD).

☿℞ USSR claimed all prisoners had been returned; disputed by Germany, 1950; Taurus (SR).

☿℞ Thieves stole Costa Rica's most prized religious relic and returned the statue seven days later, 1950; Taurus.

☿℞ Justice Department filed suit against California oil companies for price-fixing, 1950; Taurus.

☿℞ US House of Representatives passed two year draft extension, 1950, Taurus.

☿℞ Two reports in JAMA revealed more cancer in heavy smokers than in those who smoke lightly, or not at all, 1950, Taurus (SD).

☿℞ NATO ministers agreed to formally end war with Germany, 1950; Virgo.

☿℞ Truman vetoed Internal Security Act; was overturned, 1950; Virgo.

☿℞ Costa Rica opened Latin America's first stock exchange, 1950; Virgo (SD).

☿℞ Dalai Lama left Lhasa for India, 1950, Capricorn (SR).

☿℞ US government hoard of rare minerals prevented introduction of color TV, 1951; Capricorn.

☿℞ Atomic Energy Commission announced first new test plans since first test, 1951; Capricorn (SD).

☿℞ British Parliament modified Witchcraft Act of 1735, 1951; Taurus.

☿℞ University of North Carolina admitted first black, who entered medical school, 1951; Taurus.

☿℞ Cal. Tech. reported discovery of rare negative proton, 1951; Taurus.

☿℞ AT&T inaugurated transcontinental microwave phone service, 1951; Virgo (SR).

☿℞ First transcontinental television network began operations, 1951; Virgo.

☿℞ Scientists formed International Astronautical Federation, believed space flight possible by the year 2000, 1951; Virgo (SD).

☿℞ Two US Air Force jets reported sighting a "flying saucer" flying along the New Jersey coast at 900 miles per hour, 1951; Virgo (SD).

☿℞ US Civil Rights Commission petitioned the UN, charging

that millions of US blacks live in "conditions making for premature death, poverty, and disease," 1951; Sagittarius.

☿℞ UN approved draft convention giving women equal political rights with men, 1952; Aries (SR).

☿℞ Atomic Energy Commission began new series of tests, 1952; Aries.

☿℞ Britain created "forbidden zone" in NW Australia for nuclear tests, 1952; Leo.

☿℞ Kashmir accepted semi-independent union with India, 1952; Leo.

☿℞ First sex change operation in Denmark (Christine Jorgensen), 1952; Sagittarius.

☿℞ Calcutta windstorms killed 35, left 15,000 homeless, caused heavy crop damage, 1953; Aries/Pisces.

☿℞ Earthquake in Turkey killed 1200 and left 50,000 homeless, 1953; Pisces.

☿℞ Salk vaccine formally certified for preventing polio, 1953; Pisces.

☿℞ Einstein disclosed formulas for a "unified field theory," 1953; Pisces.

☿℞ Dag Hammerskjold nominated by UN Security Council, agreed to become Secretary-General, 1953; Pisces (SD).

☿℞ Population Reference Bureau study release warned US population growth is "mining our fields, forests, and water resources at a suicidal rate," 1953; Leo (SR).

☿℞ UNICEF became permanent UN agency, 1953; Leo.

☿℞ Korean armistice signed, 1953; Leo.

☿℞ Iranian 12-day heat wave ended after temperatures of up to 181 degrees F. causing 158 deaths; floods then caused over 700 deaths, 1953; Leo/Cancer.

☿℞ US ratified United Nations charter, 1953; Cancer.

☿℞ University of California announced first successful photographing of the polio virus, 1953; Scorpio.

☿℞ French troops seized Dienbienphu with intention of holding it, 1953; Scorpio.

☿℞ British Natural History Museum authorities proclaimed 1911 "Piltdown Man" a hoax, 1953; Scorpio.

☿℞ Harvard announced that corn originated in the Western Hemisphere, not Asia, 1954; Pisces.

☿℞ US exploded second H-bomb at Bikini Atoll, 1954; Pisces.

☿℞ French cabinet accepted Vietnam cease-fire, 1954; Pisces.

☿℞ Eisenhower promised no US conflict in Vietnam, 1954; Pisces.

☿℞ Salk/Sabin polio vaccine dispute aired, 1954; Pisces.

☿℞ Studebaker and Packard, last independent auto makers, merged, 1954; Cancer (SR).

☿℞ Analog computer began commercial operation at Princeton, 1954; Cancer.

☿℞ First jet transport built in US, the Boeing 707, tested in Seattle, 1954; Cancer (SD).

☿℞ Women given the right to vote in Peru, 1954; Scorpio.

☿℞ Comics Code Authority imposed, 1954; Scorpio.

☿℞ Ernest Hemingway awarded Nobel Prize for Literature, 1954; Scorpio.

☿℞ Robert (Tamara) Rees revealed his Amsterdam sex change operation, 1954; Libra (SD).

☿℞ VP Nixon began "goodwill tour" of Central America, 1955; Aquarius (SR).

☿℞ New series of atomic tests began in Nevada, 1955; Aquarius.

☿℞ General Electric reported first production of synthetic diamonds, 1955; Aquarius.

☿℞ Los Angeles banned violent crime comics, 1955; Aquarius.

☿℞ USSR urged for universal nuclear disarmament, 1955; Aquarius.

☿℞ Congress extended Selective Service Act for 4 years, 1955, Aquarius.

☿℞ President Eisenhower presented ten-year Interstate Highway plan, 1955; Aquarius (SD).

☿℞ IRS seized 60,000 gallon still, largest bootleg plant found since Prohibition, 1955; Gemini.

☿℞ Military revolt and burning of Catholic Churches after Juan Peron was excommunicated, 1955; Gemini.

☿℞ Longest eclipse (7 min. 7.8 sec.) in 1200 years over SE Asia, 1955; Gemini.

☿℞ James Dean died in an auto accident, 1955; Libra (SR).

☿℞ France walked out of UN over Algerian dispute, 1955; Libra (SR).

☿℞ Sweden ended 21 years of liquor rationing, 1955; Libra (SR).

☿℞ Argentine government lifted state of siege imposed by Peron in 1951, 1955; Libra (SR).

☿℞ First solar battery demonstrated by Bell Labs, 1955; Libra.

☿℞ News media prevented accidental publication revealing every US airbase in the whole world, 1955; Libra.

☿℞ Punjab flooding killed 225, destroyed 7000 villages, put 5.6 million acres underwater, destroyed $63 million in crops, 1955; Libra.

☿℞ USSR completed the release of more than 1700 German POWs, 1955; Libra.

☿℞ Jonas Salk's anti-polio vaccine program extended with increased funding, 1956; Aquarius/Capricorn.

☿℞ Western Europe's most severe cold wave in 20th century, killed 173 in 5 days, 1956; Aquarius/Capricorn.

☿℞ US Senator Symington asserted US-USSR missile gap with USSR ahead, 1956; Capricorn.

☿℞ Chilean Army scaled 24,284 ft. Mt. Ojos del Salado; measurements taken prove it higher than Mt. Aconcagua, 1956; Capricorn (SD).

☿℞ Great Britain announced successful atomic test, 1956; Gemini (SR).

☿℞ Hitchcock's "The Man Who Knew Too Much" premiered in NYC, 1956; Gemini (SR).

☿℞ Senator Symington announced now we have an unfavorable bomber gap, 1956; Gemini.

☿℞ Anti-neutron discovery announced, 1956; Libra (SR).

☿℞ Vito Sala, listed as AWOL since 1945, reported back for duty after recovering from amnesia, 1956; Libra.

☿℞ Chou-En-Lai said USSR/Chinese friendship "eternal and unbreakable," 1957; Capricorn.

☿℞ First US ship passed through Suez Canal since it was closed, 1957; Taurus (SR).

☿℞ Women voted for first time in Tunisia, 1957, Taurus.

☿℞ Dr. Joseph Kennedy, co-discoverer of Plutonium, died at age 40 of cancer, 1957; Taurus.

☿℞ British Pacific Ocean hydrogen bomb test, 1957; Taurus.

☿℞ Massachusetts reversed 1692 witchcraft conviction of six Salem women, 1957; Virgo.

☿℞ Governor O. Faubus ordered Arkansas National Guard to keep nine black children out of Little Rock High School, 1957; Virgo.

☿℞ First nuclear chain reaction in Latin America set off in Brazil, 1957; Virgo.

☿℞ First nuclear reactor in Japan began to produce current, 1957; Virgo (SD).

☿℞ FCC announced it would accept applications for subscription TV permits, 1957; Virgo (SD).

☿℞ British House of Commons approved program to establish British nuclear missile bases, 1957; Capricorn.

☿℞ Spanish parliament granted women the right to control their own property, 1958; Aries.

☿℞ Dean of UCLA medical school said there was no evidence atomic radiation had any genetic effect on humans or animals, 1958; Aries.

☿℞ Association of American Indian Affairs charged that BIA policy sought to erase the "Indian problem by liquidating the Indians," 1958; Aries.

☿℞ Nixon began disastrous 18-day "goodwill tour" of Latin America, 1958; Aries (SD).

☿℞ US began Marshall Islands nuclear tests, 1958; Aries (SD).

☿℞ China attacked Taiwan, 1958; Virgo (SR).

☿℞ Nautilus, US atomic sub, sailed under North Pole, 1958; Virgo (SR).

☿℞ USSR agreed to supply China with nuclear weapons, missiles, reactors, 1958; Virgo.

☿℞ US proposed, USSR accepted Geneva talks on nuclear test ban, 1958; Virgo.

☿℞ US, USSR, UK approved first four articles of a draft test ban treaty, 1958; Sagittarius.

☿℞ First domestic jet passenger service in US started, 1958; Sagittarius.

☿℞ Mao Tse-Tung retired as head of Chinese government, 1958; Sagittarius (SD).

☿℞ Tibetan revolt against Chinese occupation of Tibet; Dalai Lama fled to India; 15,000 Tibetans deported to forced labor camps, 1959; Aries (SR).

☿℞ Dep't of Defense described nuclear fallout as "greater in the US than in any other area of the world"; Linus Pauling charged nuclear detonations would cause many thousands of birth defects and cases of leukemia, bone cancer, 1959; Aries (SR).

☿℞ Eisenhower extended peacetime draft four more years, 1959; Aries.

☿℞ Oklahoma repealed prohibition after 51 years, 1959; Aries.

☿℞ Diaries of Irish patriot Roger Casement, hanged as a spy in WW I, were opened to the public for the first time, 1959; Leo.

☿℞ United Nations unanimously approved "Declaration of the Rights of the Child" as written by the UN Commission on Human Rights, 1959; Sagittarius.

☿℞ Joint US/USSR nuclear research program agreement signed, 1959; Sagittarius.

☿℞ Antarctica set aside as a scientific preserve free from military activities, 1959; Scorpio.

☿℞ Two Moroccan earthquakes, a tidal wave, and flash fire killed 12,000 and left 45,000 homeless, 1960; Pisces (SR).

☿℞ North Vietnam protested US efforts to make Laos a "virtual US military base," 1960; Pisces (SR).

☿℞ Black students at Tuskeegee launched boycott protesting 1957 Alabama law excluding blacks as residents and voters, 1960; Pisces (SR).

☿℞ US Supreme Court upheld NY state's right to force the Tuscarora Indians to sell their tribal lands to the state, 1960; Pisces.

☿℞ San Antonio, already having integrated its public transportation, became first major southern US city to open variety store lunch counters to blacks, 1960; Pisces.

☿℞ South Korean President Rhee reelected without opposition to fourth 4-year term, 1960; Pisces.

☿℞ Fourth US satellite launch failure in seven weeks, 1960; Pisces (SD).

☿℞ China apologized to Nepal for attacking its border "mistakenly," 1960; Leo (SR).

☿℞ Israel announced completion of first nuclear reactor, 1960; Leo (SR).

☿℞ A record 442 Americans died in auto accidents over July 4 weekend, 1960; Leo (SR).

☿℞ Tribal warfare, civil strife, violent mutinies during Congo's first week of independence; dozens killed, hundreds wounded, 1960; Cancer.

☿℞ Officers of S. Korean government confessed to extensive rigging of March 15th S. Korean elections, 1960; Cancer.

☿℞ Hughes Aircraft Corp. announced first laser, 1960; Cancer.

☿℞ Record distributors payola scandal reported by the FTC, 1960; Cancer.

☿℞ JFK nominated for US President, 1960; Cancer.

☿℞ Nixon nominated for US President, 1960; Cancer (SD).

☿℞ Rev. Dr. Martin Luther King released from Georgia state prison, one day after Senator John F. Kennedy promised to intervene on his behalf, 1960; Scorpio (SR).

☿℞ Nobel Peace Prize committee announced there would be no award, 1960; Scorpio (SR).

☿℞ Great Britain agreeed to US nuclear sub bases in Scotland, 1960; Scorpio.

☿℞ JFK won presidency, 1960; Scorpio.

☿℞ *Lady Chatterley's Lover* ruled not obscene in London, 1960; Scorpio.

☿℞ US Supreme Court ruled Tuskeegee boundary law excluding blacks from voting was unconstitutional, 1960; Scorpio.

☿℞ Seven year legal suit against Standard Oil and Gulf Oil

ended with both agreeing to refrain from price fixing and market control practices, 1960; Scorpio.

☿℞ First US atomic submarine armed with nuclear missiles launched, 1960; Scorpio (SD).

☿℞ Ex-Premier Lumumba of Congo killed under mysterious circumstances, leading to civil war and UN intervention, 1961; Pisces (SR).

☿℞ Major U.S. auto makers announced seatbelts would be standard in 1962 models, 1961; Pisces/Aquarius.

☿℞ Peace Corps established by President John F. Kennedy, 1961; Aquarius.

☿℞ Castro reversed himself, demanded 1000 farm tractors instead of 500, in exchange for Bay of Pigs captives, 1961; Cancer (SR).

☿℞ Rudolph Nureyev, ballet star, asked for political asylum, 1961; Cancer (SR).

☿℞ Great Britain ended its 62-year protectorate of Kuwait, pledging to defend Kuwait's independence; Iraq claimed sovereignty over Kuwait; Kuwait and Great Britain reject the claim; Iraq sent troops to the border, and then claimed it never intended to use force, 1961; Cancer.

☿℞ First experimental water desalinization plant in US put into operation, 1961; Cancer.

☿℞ Adolph Eichmann concluded twelve days of testimony claiming "I've never killed anyone," 1961; Cancer.

☿℞ First Dominican Republic anti-government demonstration in 31 years erupted in violence, 1961; Cancer.

☿℞ Anti-US protests in Nigeria over postcard from Peace Corps member describing living conditions there as primitive and squalid; she later apologized for "her senseless letter," 1961; Scorpio.

☿℞ Serious fighting in Rwanda between Bahutu and Watusi tribesmen, 1961; Scorpio.

☿℞ Nobel Peace Prize awarded posthumously to Dag Hammarskjold, 1961; Libra.

☿℞ USSR detonated 30 megaton nuclear bomb, largest in history, 1961; Libra.

☿℞ Communist Party Congress ordered Stalin's body removed from its place next to Lenin in the Red Square Mausoleum, 1961; Libra.

☿℞ US Moon launch missed target by 22,000 miles, 1962; Aquarius (SR).

☿℞ John F. Kennedy said he sent no US combat troops to South Vietnam; Nixon announced his full support of the administration's commitment to "step up the build-up of troops," 1962; Aquarius.

☿℞ Jamaica gained independence, 1962; Aquarius.

☿℞ John Glenn went into orbit, 1962; Aquarius.

☿℞ Third and last Antichrist of this age supposedly born (according to Nostradamus), 1962; Aquarius.

☿℞ US House of Representatives passed a bill requiring interstate companies to pay equal wages to men and women doing equal work in the same plant, 1962; Gemini (SR).

☿℞ Adolph Eichmann hanged, 1962; Gemini.

☿℞ Buck O'Neil, signed by the Chicago Cubs, became the first black coach in Major League Baseball history, 1962; Gemini.

☿℞ Atlanta Art Association chartered jetliner crashed in Paris, killing 130, worst single plane disaster in history, 1962; Gemini.

☿℞ First successful escape from Alcatraz, 1962; Gemini.

☿℞ Governor Ross Barnett personally blocked James Meredith from registering at the University of Mississippi, was charged with contempt; JFK sent in federal troops, and Meredith was enrolled a week later amid violent riots, 1962; Libra (SR).

☿℞ Flash flooding in Spain killed 445, worst national disaster in modern Spanish history, 1962; Libra.

☿℞ First non US/USSR satellite launched by Canada, 1962; Libra.

☿℞ Dutch rule over New Guinea was officially ended, 1962; Libra.

☿℞ *The Brooklyn Eagle*, a New York City newspaper founded

in 1841, resumed operations after a seven year shutdown, 1962; Libra (SD).

☿℞ Robert F. Kennedy denied that US promised air cover for Bay of Pigs invasion; anti-Castro Revolutionary Council said US military officers guaranteed US "air support"; Senator Goldwater called for an investigation, 1963; Capricorn.

☿℞ First members of football's Hall of Fame named, 1963; Capricorn.

☿℞ Birmingham, Alabama race riots and bombing, 1963; Gemini (SR).

☿℞ Senate passed administration bill requiring equal pay for equal work regardless of sex, 1963; Taurus.

☿℞ Astronaut Gordon Cooper blasted off after radar malfunction caused delay on the final mission of the Project Mercury space program; was forced to do a manual reentry because of automatic guidance system malfunction, 1963; Taurus.

☿℞ Year old rumors about Pope John XXIII's stomach cancer were confirmed, 1963; Taurus.

☿℞ Fischer quintuplets born in San Diego, 1963; Libra.

☿℞ Black church bombing in Birmingham killed four children, led to nationwide demonstrations, 1963; Libra/Virgo.

☿℞ John F. Kennedy unexpectedly announced to UN a proposal for a joint US/USSR manned lunar expedition, 1963; Virgo.

☿℞ US Senate ratified US/USSR/UK nuclear test ban treaty, 1963; Virgo.

☿℞ Joe Valachi described the Mafia's structure and operations to the U.S. Senate, 1963; Virgo (SD).

☿℞ 1.25 million West Berliners given special passes to visit relatives for the first time since August 1962; 1963; Capricorn (SR).

☿℞ Dallas District Attorney Wade reported no collusion between Jack Ruby and the Dallas Police Department in Oswald's slaying, 1964; Capricorn.

☿℞ Pope Paul VI ended first papal journey outside Italy since 1809 as well as first air flight ever made by a Pope, 1964; Capricorn.

☿℞ Second mistrial of Byron de la Beckwith in the 1963 murder of Medgar Evars, 1964; Taurus (SR).

☿℞ Socialist government of Saskatchewan, in power over twenty years, was ousted by the Liberal Party, 1964; Taurus.

☿℞ J. Edgar Hoover testimony released saying Communist influence was in the "Negro movement," 1964; Taurus.

☿℞ First nine-inning, no-hit loss in Major League Baseball history, 1964; Taurus.

☿℞ Greek government granted amnesty to 421 communists jailed in the late 1940's, 1964; Taurus.

☿℞ General Electric paid $26.5 million to settle 1960 price fixing suit, 1964; Taurus.

☿℞ Nine major US cigarette makers adopted a ban on youth oriented advertising, 1964; Taurus.

☿℞ Indonesian government marked "Education Day" by burning 500 European language books, 1964; Taurus.

☿℞ Rockefeller Institute announced first successful gene transplant for a specific hereditary trait, 1964; Taurus.

☿℞ The full Roman Catholic Mass was celebrated in English for the first time, 1964; Virgo.

☿℞ Beatles at the Hollywood Bowl, 1964; Virgo.

☿℞ Three Cuban exiles attempted and failed to bazooka the UN during Che Guevarra's talk; busted after eleven days, 1964; Capricorn.

☿℞ A U-2 crash near Tucson forced US government to disclose it had been training Nationalist Chinese pilots, 1964; Sagittarius.

☿℞ Communists blocked or closed the Berlin autobahn six times, 1965; Aries.

☿℞ US government opposed smog control devices, 1965; Aries.

☿℞ US House of Representatives hired its first black page, 1965; Aries.

☿℞ West Germany paid its final installment of WW II reparations to Israel, 1965; Aries.

☿℞ US/USSR underground nuclear tests, 1965; Aries.

☿℞ USSR canceled all debt owed by collective farms, 1965; Aries (SD).

☿℞ Iraq troops and planes attacked Kurds, 1965; Aries (SD).

☿℞ Radar studies showed Mercury was rotating faster than was thought, 1965; Aries (SD).

☿℞ USSR conducted underground nuclear test, 1965; Virgo/Leo (SR).

☿℞ Draft quotas went up sharply for September and October 1965; Virgo/Leo (SR).

☿℞ President Johnson denied there was a "substantial split" in US opinion about Vietnam, 1965; Leo.

☿℞ Watts riots began in Los Angeles; 34 die, over 1100 injured, 1965; Leo.

☿℞ Gemini 5 astronauts lost power, regained it the next day, and went on to set a longevity mark, 1965; Leo.

☿℞ President Johnson signed the Voting Rights Act, 1965; Leo.

☿℞ US/USSR conducted multiple underground nuclear tests, 1965; Sagittarius.

☿℞ Kurds reported a new offensive by the Iraq government, 1965; Sagittarius.

☿℞ Roman Catholic and Eastern Orthodox Churches renounced the anathema of 1054, excommunicating the leaders of each church, 1965; Sagittarius.

☿℞ Watts riots in Los Angeles erupted again, 1966; Aries.

☿℞ Gemini 8 astronauts Armstrong and Scott staged first docking of orbiting spacecraft; were forced down the next day after losing control of their craft, 1966; Aries.

☿℞ Soviet Luna 10, first human-made object to attain lunar orbit, 1966; Pisces (SD).

☿℞ Fighting, looting, shooting, and firebomb riots occurred in Chicago, Brooklyn, Cleveland, Omaha, Kalamazoo, Lansing, and Troy, NY, 1966; Leo (SR).

☿℞ Argentina began talks with Great Britain about the Falkland Islands, 1966; Leo.

☿℞ Guatemala gave amnesty to political prisoners arrested since November 1960, 1966; Leo.

☿℞ USSR underground nuclear tests, 1966; Leo.

☿℞ US postponed the launch of Gemini 12, final Gemini mission flight, for one day; Lovell and Aldrin multiple spacewalks, 1966; Sagittarius (SR).

☿℞ US automakers recalled 500,000 cars for defects, 1966; Scorpio.

☿℞ David Ferrie, prime suspect in the Garrison assassination investigation, is found dead; New Orleans coroner declares he died of natural causes; District Attorney Garrison called his death a suicide, 1967; Pisces (SR).

☿℞ A Federal jury indicted nineteen in the 1964 murder of three civil rights workers, and twelve in the 1966 murder of Vernon Dahmer, 1967; Pisces.

☿℞ LBJ proposed a draft lottery to replace selective service procedures, 1967; Pisces (SD).

☿℞ French conducted nuclear tests in the Pacific, China conducts H-bomb tests, 1967; Cancer (SR).

☿℞ Looting, sniper fire, riots, firebombings in Buffalo, Newark, and Cairo, Illinois, 1967; Cancer (started SR, finished SD).

☿℞ US lost contact with Surveyor 4 just before it landed on the moon; gave up efforts to recontact after two days, 1967; Cancer.

☿℞ Federal jury convicted seven whites of conspiracy in 1964 murder of three civil rights workers in Mississippi, 1967; Scorpio (SR).

☿℞ US conducted multiple underground tests, 1967; Scorpio.

☿℞ For the first time since 1954, opposition parties were allowed to campaign in a Paraguay election, 1968; Pisces/Aquarius.

☿℞ US nuclear test in Nevada, 1968; Aquarius.

☿℞ Robert Kennedy assassinated in Los Angeles, 1968; Cancer (SR).

☿℞ US multiple underground nuclear tests in Nevada; 1968; Cancer (SR).

☿℞ French conducted nuclear tests in the Pacific, 1968; Cancer (SR).

☿℞ Scotland Yard arrested James Earl Ray in London, 1968; Cancer.

☿℞ UN approved nuclear non-proliferation treaty, 1968; Cancer.

☿℞ US Congress made US flag desecration a crime, 1968; Gemini.

☿℞ USSR conducted underground nuclear tests in Asia, 1968; Gemini (tests end SD).

☿℞ Redwood National Park established in northern California, 1968; Scorpio (SR).

☿℞ US conducted nuclear tests in Nevada, 1968; Scorpio (SR).

☿℞ Quebec separatist party created, 1968; Libra.

☿℞ Nixon inaugurated as President, 1969; Aquarius (SR).

☿℞ Astronauts Eugene Cernan, Tom Stafford, and John Young blasted off aboard Apollo 10, 1969; Gemini (SR).

☿℞ Apollo 10 lunar module separated from command module and flew to within nine miles of the moon as a rehearsal for the moon landing, 1969; Gemini.

☿℞ US captured Apha Mountain in one of the bloodiest battles of the war; abandoned it eight days later, 1969; Gemini.

☿℞ USSR conducted underground tests, 1969; Gemini.

☿℞ Pentagon warned arms contractors that unrealistically low bids would no longer be tolerated, 1969; Gemini.

☿℞ USSR/US conducted underground nuclear tests, 1969; Libra.

☿℞ US/USSR treaty banning nuclear weapons on the seabed, 1969; Virgo (SD).

☿℞ Book dealer Hans Kraus donated 1504 Amerigo Vespucci letter to US Library of Congress, 1970; Capricorn.

☿℞ GM President Cole predicted an almost pollution-free car will be built by 1980, 1970; Capricorn.

☿℞ Diana Ross made her last appearance with the Supremes, 1970; Capricorn.

☿℞ Israelis uncovered first evidence of Roman troops razing Jerusalem in A.D. 70, 1970; Capricorn.

☿℞ Curt Flood filed anti-trust suit against baseball's reserve clause, 1970; Capricorn.

☿℞ 33,000 Argentinean medical doctors strike for 24 hours, 1970; Capricorn (SD).

☿℞ US government began investigation of Alaska oil slick that killed thousands of birds, two whales, and other animals, 1970; Taurus (SR).

☿℞ French scientists announced first nuclear heart pacemaker, 1970; Taurus (SR).

☿℞ 3 operators of an anti-war coffeehouse near Ft. Jackson, SC got six year sentences for "operating a public nuisance," 1970; Taurus.

☿℞ Nixon announced he was sending troops to Cambodia; worldwide protests followed, 1970; Taurus.

☿℞ "Sesame Street" banned in Mississippi "because of its racial overtones," 1970; Taurus.

☿℞ Ohio National Guard opened fire on Kent State students, killing four and wounding nine, 1970; Taurus.

☿℞ 448 colleges and universities closed or under strike, 1970; Taurus.

☿℞ Iceland's largest volcano erupted for first time in 23 years, 1970; Taurus.

☿℞ Brazil denied there is torture in its prisons; refused to allow journalists to verify treatment of prisoners, 1970; Taurus.

☿℞ Two students killed at Jackson State University by police during student protests, 1970; Taurus.

☿℞ USSR restored its Ministry of Justice, abolished in 1956, 1970; Virgo (SR).

☿℞ First known cholera epidemic south of the Sahara, 1970; Virgo (SR).

☿℞ NASA canceled second lunar landing because of budget cuts, 1970; Virgo.

☿℞ Huge oil slick moved through St. Lawrence toward New Brunswick, 1970; Virgo.

☿℞ US Congress approved clean air bill requiring cars to be 90 percent pollution-free by 1976, 1970; Capricorn (SR).

☿℞ Israeli archeologists reported discovering the cornerstone of the Temple destroyed by the Romans in A.D. 70, as well as the first authenticated evidence of a crucifixion in the Holy Land, 1971; Sagittarius.

☿℞ China admitted Western newsmen for first time since 1949, 1971; Taurus (SR).

☿℞ Nixon relaxed 20-year US trade embargo with China, 1971; Taurus.

☿℞ 200,000 anti-war activists marched in Washington DC, 1971; Aries.

☿℞ US draft law extended for 2+ years, 1971; Aries.

☿℞ US Attorney General John Mitchell quashed grand jury investigation of Kent State massacre, 1971; Virgo (SR).

☿℞ Unexpected Nixon freeze on wages, prices, rents; ended convertibility of dollars into gold; Dow Jones average recorded biggest single day gain in history, 1971; Virgo.

☿℞ US informs International Monetary Fund it would no longer settle transactions in gold; IMF recognized US dollar as a floating currency, 1971; Virgo.

☿℞ US Navy tanker spilled 230,000 gallons of oil on California coast, created 65-mile slick, 1971; Virgo.

☿℞ Canada recommended legalization of marijuana and hashish, 1971; Virgo.

☿℞ US government dropped charges against 800+ May Day antiwar demonstrators, arrested previous May 2nd, with Mercury stationary direct, 1971; Virgo.

☿℞ Largest General Motors recall in history (6.68 million vehicles), 1971; Sagittarius.

☿℞ Nixon formally devalued US dollar, sending it plunging on international money markets, 1971; Sagittarius.

☿℞ Movie *Slaughterhouse 5* released in NYC, 1972; Aries (SR).

☿℞ National Commission on Drug Abuse recommended all criminal penalties for private use of marijuana be abolished, 1972; Aries (SR).

☿℞ USSR underground nuclear test, 1972; Aries.

☿℞ Further devaluation of US dollar, 1972; Aries.

☿℞ Congress sent the ERA to the states for ratification, 1972; Aries.

☿℞ The US, USSR, and 70 other nations banned chemical warfare, 1972; Aries.

☿℞ General Motors recalled 130,000 1972 model cars, 1972; Aries.

☿℞ First game of baseball season canceled by strike; first strike in MLB history ended eight days later, with Mercury SD, 1972; Aries.

☿℞ Associated Press released details of Tuskeegee syphilis study, where hundreds of blacks were deliberately not treated for syphilis for decades, 1972; Leo (SR).

☿℞ FBI opened investigations into the Committee to Re-elect the President's break-in at the Democratic Party headquarters at the Watergate hotel, 1972; Leo.

☿℞ The last US combat troops left Vietnam; 43,500 service personnel remained, 1972; Leo.

☿℞ 2 black students killed at Southern University protest by police, 1972; Sagittarius (SR).

☿℞ 65 Belfast priests accused the British army of shooting civilians to provoke IRA action, 1972; Sagittarius.

☿℞ Supreme Court ruled that computer programs cannot be patented, 1972; Sagittarius.

☿℞ Chicago 7 trial verdicts overturned due to judicial impropriety, 1972; Sagittarius.

☿℞ First public admission by US Air Force of losing a B-52 to enemy fire, 1972; Sagittarius.

☿℞ USSR began operating the first commercial atomic fast-breeder reactor; US then announced a major breakthrough promising an "inexhaustible supply of nuclear energy," 1972; Scorpio.

☿℞ US/USSR agreement for construction of new embassies (the Russians got one of the choicest spots in Washington DC; the US's was bugged from the ground up!), 1972; Scorpio (SD).

☿℞ Judge Sirica ordered the political motivation for Watergate break-in investigated, 1972; Scorpio (SD).

☿℞ CIA agent, in Chinese prison since 1952, returned to US, 1973; Pisces.

☿℞ Nixon invoked executive privilege to prevent staff from testifying before Congress, 1973; Pisces.

☿℞ Cease-fire agreement reached at Wounded Knee, 1973; Pisces.

☿℞ Iraq and Kuwait troops clashed on disputed border, 1973; Pisces.

☿℞ First round of Watergate sentencing, 1973; Pisces.

☿℞ Nixon refused to testify, denied access to his papers, 1973; Leo (SR).

☿℞ Bahamas became independent, ending 300 years of British rule, 1973; Leo.

☿℞ Nolan Ryan became first baseball pitcher in 21 years to throw two no-hitters in one season, 1973; Leo/Cancer.

☿℞ Alexander Butterfield testimony confirmed about Nixon oval office recording system and tapes; Nixon refused to give Congress the Oval Office tapes, 1973; Cancer.

☿℞ Elks Club rescinded 105 year racial ban, 1973; Cancer.

☿℞ Asia, Canada, Sweden protested French South Pacific atomic tests; USSR detonated major nuclear device, 1973; Cancer.

☿℞ Nixon order of secret 1969–1970 bombing of Cambodia confirmed; further bombings ruled illegal, 1973; Cancer.

☿℞ Nixon impeachment resolution "for high crimes and misdemeanors," 1973; Cancer (SD).

☿℞ Chicago 7 acquitted, 1973; Scorpio.

☿℞ War Powers Act passed by Congress, 1973; Scorpio.

☿℞ Second round of Watergate sentencing, 1973; Scorpio.

☿℞ New evidence presented that humans lived in North America 250,000 years ago, 1973; Scorpio.

☿℞ Nixon declared "I am not a crook" at Disney World, 1973; Scorpio.

☿℞ Oil companies charged with manipulating gas shortages to drive up prices, 1974; Pisces.

☿℞ US underground nuclear test in Nevada, 1974; Pisces.

☿℞ Judge Sirica handed down indictments to Haldeman, Erhlichman, John Mitchell, four other top aides, 1974; Pisces.

☿℞ Worst jumbo jet disaster in history; 345 dead in Paris, 1974; Pisces/Aquarius.

☿℞ France and China conducted atmospheric nuclear tests, 1974; Cancer (SR).

☿℞ North Korea sank South Korean gunboat, 1974; Cancer.

☿℞ Liz Taylor and Richard Burton divorced, 1974; Cancer.

☿℞ Juan Peron died in Argentina, Maria Estela Peron became first female Chief of State in the Americas, 1974; Cancer.

☿℞ USSR nuclear test measured 5.2 on the Richter scale, 1974; Cancer.

☿℞ Human fossils over three million years old discovered in Ethiopia, 1974; Scorpio.

☿℞ President Ford repealed 1955 Formosa Resolution which pledged US to defend Taiwan, 1974; Scorpio/Libra.

☿℞ Muhammed Ali resigned heavyweight boxing title, 1974; Libra.

☿℞ President Ford signed Solar Energy Research and Development Act, 1974; Libra.

☿℞ Severe earthquake in Guatemala/Honduras killed over 22,000, 1975; Aquarius.

☿℞ General Motors recalled 220,000 cars for a wheel defect, 1975; Aquarius.

☿℞ Alaska legalized home pot use, 1975; Gemini (SR).

☿℞ NY Times reported Kissinger's "New World Economic Order," 1975; Gemini (SR).

☿℞ Nolan Ryan threw fourth no-hit game; equaled Kofax's MLB record, 1975; Gemini.

☿℞ Federal Trade Commission charged Hertz and National Car Rental with conspiracy to price fix, 1975; Gemini.

☿℞ Two dental professors given patent for a drill-less method of removing tooth decay, 1975; Gemini.

☿℞ On-going conflict about gays in the military reported, 1975; Gemini.

☿℞ Rockefeller Inquiry found no pattern of illegal activity by the CIA, 1975; Gemini.

☿℞ NBC reported computer files on over 600,000 anti-war protesters existed at the CIA, FBI, DIA, and NSA as well as numerous universities, 1975; Gemini.

☿℞ Egypt re-opened Suez Canal exactly eight years after they closed it, 1975; Gemini.

☿℞ First ship to sail directly from Egypt to Israel since 1948, 1975; Libra (SR).

☿℞ Previously secret Pentagon-Middle East weapons contracts revealed, 1975; Libra (SR).

☿℞ First ascent of Mt. Everest's SW face, 1975; Libra (SR).

☿℞ Andrei Sakharov won Nobel Peace Prize, 1975; Libra.

☿℞ Liz Taylor and Richard Burton remarried in Botswana after fourteen-month divorce, 1975; Libra (see 1974 Mercury Retrograde in Cancer).

☿℞ Pope Paul VI canonized Oliver Plunkett, Irish Archbishop executed for treason in 1681, 1975; Libra.

☿℞ France began first anti-smoking drive, 1975; Libra.

☿℞ "First Women's Bank" opened in NYC after more than a year of delays, 1975; Libra.

☿℞ FDA banned red dye #2, 1976; Aquarius.

☿℞ Cambodia forcibly removed hundreds of thousands from cities to rural areas, 1976; Aquarius.

☿℞ *New York Times* and *Washington Post* published stories about questionable CIA activities, 1976; Aquarius.

☿℞ China conducted nuclear test, 1976; Aquarius.

☿℞ George Bush confirmed as Director of the CIA, 1976; Capricorn.

☿℞ Prison identified where, in 399 B.C., Socrates drank hemlock and died, 1976; Capricorn.

☿℞ Senate Intelligence Committee staff report released saying FBI conducted wiretaps for Presidents Johnson and Nixon, 1976; Gemini (SR).

☿℞ Scholars displayed bronze and jewelry artifacts from Thailand that predate the earliest known bronze age relics, 1976; Gemini.

☿℞ France and West Germany agreed to join fast breeder nuclear technology, 1976; Gemini.

☿℞ Typhoon Olga struck the Philippines producing four days of floods, 215 deaths, left 630,000 homeless, 1976; Gemini/Taurus.

☿℞ International Energy Agency agreed on eighteen nation nuclear and petroleum cooperation, 1976; Taurus.

☿℞ France agreed to build nuclear plants in Iran and South Africa (the first in Africa), 1976; Taurus.

☿℞ US/USSR treaty limiting the size of underground nuclear tests, 1976; Taurus.

☿℞ Seven oil companies indicted on price fixing charges, 1976; Taurus (SD).

☿℞ Chairman Mao Tse-tung of China died, 1976; Libra (SR).

☿℞ New York State and General Electric agreed to end PBP pollution of the Hudson River, 1976; Libra (SR).

☿℞ FDA approved ten cold medicines for public sale; Advisory Panel said nothing can "prevent, cure, or shorten the common cold," 1976; Libra (SR).

☿℞ US/USSR banned major environmental warfare, 1976; Libra.

☿℞ National Academy of Sciences called for regulation of CFCs, 1976; Libra.

☿℞ Typhoon Fran in Japan killed over 100, left 325,000 homeless after 100 mph winds and five feet of rain in five days, 1976; Libra.

☿℞ US Episcopal Church approved the ordination of women, 1976; Libra.

☿℞ US House of Representatives created a committee to investigate the assassinations of John F. Kennedy and Martin Luther King, 1976; Libra.

☿℞ Six days of earthquakes in Italy left four dead, 20,000 homeless, 1976; Libra.

☿℞ Social Democratic Party in Sweden suffered first defeat in 44 years, 1976; Libra/Virgo.

☿℞ Episcopalian Bishops approved the first major revisions in

427 years to the Book of Common Prayer, 1976; Libra/Virgo.

☿℞ First Ford/Carter debate; technical problems led to loss of sound for twenty-seven minutes, 1976; Virgo.

☿℞ FDA banned Red dye #4 and carbon black, 1976; Virgo.

☿℞ CDC held Sabin's live-virus polio vaccine responsible for over half of recent polio cases; Dr. Jonas Salk contended Sabin vaccine caused 140 polio cases since 1960, 1976; Virgo.

☿℞ Frozen water found on Mars, 1976; Virgo.

☿℞ Rhodesia shifted to first biracial rulership, 1976; Virgo.

☿℞ China nuclear weapons tests undertaken to boost morale after Mao's death, 1976; Virgo.

☿℞ UN proposed assisting developing nations in building nuclear energy potential, 1976; Virgo.

☿℞ Congress cleared first major revision of US copyright law since 1909, 1976; Virgo (SD).

☿℞ First right-to-die law enacted by any US state, 1976; Virgo (SD).

☿℞ Carter imposed conflict of interest code to stop government and business "revolving door," 1977; Capricorn.

☿℞ Abu Daoud, 1972 Olympic terrorist, caught by police in Paris; rejecting West German and Israeli demands, he was set free Jan 11; Israel recalled its French ambassador, 1977; Capricorn.

☿℞ *Newsday* reported 1971 CIA plot to spread Swine Flu to Cuba, 1977; Capricorn.

☿℞ First Tien An Men Square gathering in China, honoring Chou En-Lai, 1977; Capricorn.

☿℞ Gary Gilmore executed in Utah, the first death penalty execution in US since 1967, 1977; Capricorn (SD).

☿℞ Israel exchanged 28 Egyptian prisoners for nine soldiers killed in 1973 and two hanged as spies in 1955, 1977; Capricorn (SD).

☿℞ Twenty-fifth Bildeberger Conference, 1977; Taurus (SR).

☿℞ First international congress on UFOs, 1977; Taurus (SR).

☿℞ Chairman of US House of Representatives assassination investigation committee charged those who oppose the investigation have CIA links, 1977; Taurus.

☿℞ Japan established their first fast breeder nuclear reactor, 1977; Taurus.

☿℞ Worst oil spill in North Sea history, 1977; Taurus.

☿℞ Discovery of quarks first announced, 1977; Taurus.

☿℞ China invited Dalai Lama to return if he accepted Communist authority, 1977; Taurus.

☿℞ Catholic bishops rescinded 930-year-old rule excommunicating divorcees who remarry without church approval, 1977; Taurus.

☿℞ Thousands protested Seabrook nuclear plant in NH on May Day; hundreds arrested were released May 13, with Mercury SD, 1977; Taurus.

☿℞ Eskimo filed revised land claim to 105,000 square miles of Canada; Mohawks gained control of 672 disputed acres in Adirondack Mountains from US government, 1977; Taurus (SD).

☿℞ US/USSR stopped South African nuclear test in the Kalahari Desert, 1977; Virgo.

☿℞ South African finance minister said South Africa would develop atomic weapons; hours later the foreign minister said South Africa would not, 1977; Virgo.

☿℞ Nixon admitted he ordered White House tapes destroyed, 1977; Virgo.

☿℞ USSR revised national anthem after twenty years of not being able to sing it, 1977; Virgo.

☿℞ US launched Voyager I the first Jupiter-Saturn space mission, 1977; Virgo.

☿℞ Canada converted their highway signs to metric system, leaving only the US, Liberia, and South Yemen using our system, 1977; Virgo.

☿℞ Pakistani President Bhutto arrested in a legal coup, 1977; Virgo.

☿℞ USSR hosted its first International Book Fair; confiscated *1984* and *Animal Farm*, 1977; Virgo.

☿℞ Steven Biko died after a week in South African police detention, 1977; Virgo.

☿℞ China tested guided nuclear missiles, 1977; Virgo.

☿℞ European space communication satellite exploded on takeoff, 1977; Virgo (SD).

☿℞ SDS leader Mark Rudd surrendered after seven years as a fugitive, 1977; Virgo (SD).

☿℞ Dutch court convicted Pieter Menten, 78, of WW II crimes; got 15-year sentence, 1977; Capricorn (SR).

☿℞ Exxon Nuclear Co. breakthrough in laser use to enrich uranium, 1977; Capricorn (SR).

☿℞ Two weeks of Cypriot, West German, French, Italian terrorist activity, 1977; Capricorn (SR) through Sagittarius.

☿℞ Over a one week period, two oil tankers collided off South Africa, spilling oil; a Swiss jet crash killed 31; Texas and Louisiana grain elevators exploded killing 18 and 35; an Iranian earthquake killed 589, 1977; Capricorn/Sagittarius.

☿℞ Canada cut economic ties with South Africa over apartheid, 1977; Capricorn.

☿℞ President Carter signed a bill prohibiting US corporations from bribing foreign officials, 1977; Capricorn.

☿℞ US resumed charter flights to Cuba for first time since 1958, 1977; Sagittarius.

☿℞ Iraq canceled Christmas, protesting Anwar Sadat's peace bid, 1977; Sagittarius.

☿℞ Begin of Israel flew to Egypt to meet with Sadat for the first time, 1977; Sagittarius.

☿℞ Paris hit by fifteen bombings over Christmas holiday, 1977; Sagittarius.

☿℞ India launched three-year total prohibition drive against alcohol, 1978; Aries (SR).

☿℞ Oil spill off Cape Cod, 1978; Aries (SR).

☿℞ Mary Simpson became the first female Anglican priest to preach at Westminster Abbey, 1978; Aries (SR).

☿℞ Carter decided to ban the neutron bomb, then reconsidered, then said it's up to how the USSR behaves, 1978; Aries.

☿℞ Nude bathing on beaches banned by Santa Barbara, 1978; Aries.

☿℞ Amid fraud charges, Marcos won control of Philippine government in first election since he imposed martial law in 1972, 1978; Aries.

☿℞ Aldo Moro kidnapped by Italian Red Brigade terrorists; a hoax reported him executed; later photos showed him alive (was executed in early May), 1978; Aries.

☿℞ South Africa was left with no diplomatic representation anywhere in the world, 1978; Aries.

☿℞ Former FBI director and high officials indicted on federal charges involving illegal FBI activity against US citizens, 1978; Aries.

☿℞ *New Scientist* reported a black hole at the center of giant galaxy M87, 1978; Aries.

☿℞ USSR was forced by Georgian protests to reinstate the Georgian language officially, 1978; Aries.

☿℞ *NY Times* reported USAF officer Dr. Ken Cooper as the originator of "the current jogging fad," 1978; Aries.

☿℞ US Senate voted to give up the Panama Canal, 1978; Aries.

☿℞ Nuclear Regulatory Agency turned down the sale of 7.6 tons of uranium to India; President Carter overrode the decision one week later, 1978; Aries.

☿℞ Arizona astronomers estimate 10–20 percent of the 100 billion stars in this galaxy have planets orbiting around them, 1978; Aries.

☿℞ First-ever mix-up in awarding the Pulitizer Prize to the wrong person, 1978; Aries.

☿℞ Love Canal evacuation; declared a disaster area, 1978; Virgo (SR).

☿℞ Pope Paul VI died of a heart attack, 1978; Virgo (SR).

☿℞ Major anti-nuclear demonstrations nationwide in US marking Hiroshima/Nagasaki; Australians agreed to sell uranium to the Philippines, 1978; Virgo (SR).

☿℞ First US House Assassination Committee public hearings on MLK, 1978; Leo.

☿℞ US currency hit all-time low against the Mark, Swiss Franc, Yen, 1978; Leo.

☿℞ First successful trans-Atlantic balloon flight ended, 1978; Leo.

☿℞ A fire in a movie theater in Abadan, Iran killed 430; the government charged it was set by Muslim extremists; this led to massive violent demonstrations that eventually became the Iranian revolution, 1978; Leo.

☿℞ Pope John Paul I became Pope (died after 34 days in office; murder rumored), 1978; Leo (SD).

☿℞ 193-year old *London Times* suspended publication, 1978; Sagittarius.

☿℞ Announcement of a new class of materials to convert sunlight to electricity economically, 1978; Sagittarius.

☿℞ New Iranian anti-Shah demonstrations ordered by Khomeni from France, national oil strikes, Americans left; Khomeni annulled all pro-Shah Iranian treaties, 1978; Sagittarius.

☿℞ Spanish voters approved new constitution establishing parliamentary monarchy, 1978; Sagittarius.

☿℞ Begin and Sadat received their Nobel Peace Prize, 1978; Sagittarius.

☿℞ Pioneer Venus space probe data implied current planetary evolution ideas need revision, 1978; Sagittarius.

☿℞ For first time, Federal Home Loan Bank allowed S & L's to offer variable rate, graduated payment, and reverse annuity mortgages, 1978; Sagittarius (SD).

☿℞ US and China announced full diplomatic relations, 1978; Sagittarius (SD).

☿℞ *The China Syndrome*, a nuclear disaster movie, opened in NYC twelve days before the Three Mile Island nuclear accident, 1979; Aries (SR).

☿℞ Camp David peace accord ending thirty years of war between Israel and Egypt signed by Sadat and Begin, 1979; Aries.

☿℞ Three Mile Island nuclear reactor accident, 1979; Aries/ Pisces.

☿℞ Ayatollah Khomeni proclaimed Iran an Islamic Republic, 1979; Pisces.

☿℞ Australia banned whaling within its 200-mile zone, 1979; Pisces.

☿℞ Spanish Premier named a Cabinet, first Constitutional government since the 30s, 1979; Pisces.

☿℞ US House Assassination Committee said a conspiracy was likely in JFK and MLK deaths, 1979; Leo (SR).

☿℞ Somoza resigned as Nicaraguan President; Sandanistas took over after seven-week civil war killing 10,000, and leaving millions homeless, 1979; Leo (SR).

☿℞ President Carter halted the withdrawal of last 32,000 troops in Korea until 1981, 1979; Leo.

☿℞ Government approval granted to allow public access to Nixon tapes, 1979; Leo.

☿℞ Steven Biko's family received out-of-court settlement for his death, 1979; Leo.

☿℞ Oil tanker sank east of Barbados; Lloyds of London's largest maritime loss, $85 million, 1979; Leo.

☿℞ Nuclear Regulatory Commission report stated Three Mile Island "was preventable despite . . . equipment failures and design inadequacies," 1979; Leo.

☿℞ 5.9 earthquake in San Francisco, strongest in fifty years; Mt. Etna in Italy erupted two times in three days, 1979; Leo.

☿℞ Israel returned Mt. Sinai to Egypt two months early, 1979; Sagittarius.

☿℞ Iran suspended payments on foreign debts; Saudi National Guard re-took Mecca's Grand Mosque held for two days by terrorists who held 50,000 hostage; hundreds of casualties, 1979; Scorpio.

☿℞ Pakistani airline crash in Saudi Arabia killed 156; New Zealand airliner crashed in Antarctica, killing 257, 1979; Scorpio.

☿℞ Power failure caused thousands of gallons of radioactive water to spill at Crystal River, FL, nuclear plant, 1980; Pisces (SR).

☿℞ France agreed to supply Iraq with weapons-grade uranium and an experimental reactor, 1980; Pisces (SR).

☿℞ First-ever US vote against Israeli settlements in UN; two days later Carter said it was a mistake resulting from a communication failure, 1980; Pisces.

☿℞ Late winter snowstorm hit US east coast; 28 inches of snow, $2 billion Florida citrus crop frozen, 1980; Pisces.

☿℞ Scientists succeeded in producing teeth in chickens, 1980; Pisces.

☿℞ A Colombian witch, running on health, money, and love, confounded political insiders by winning two city council seats and two state assembly seats in Bogota and Medellin, 1980; Pisces.

☿℞ Italian magistrates ordered 25 arrested in the kidnap-murder of Aldo Moro, 1980; Pisces.

☿℞ Penobscot tribe approved $81.5 million settlement against Maine over illegal land seizures, 1980; Pisces.

☿℞ Massive 70s Soviet caviar fraud reported; senior officials and hundreds of bureaucrats indicted, 1980; Pisces.

☿℞ USSR admitted to anthrax outbreak in April 1979, claimed it was tainted meat; US officials suspect deaths were due to illegal biological warfare experiments going awry, 1980; Pisces (SD).

☿℞ US Supreme Court required that those responsible for an oil spill must report it, even if it incriminates them, 1980; Cancer (SR).

☿℞ President Carter signed draft registration bill for 19- and 20-year olds; authorized Vietnam Memorial, 1980; Cancer (SR).

☿℞ Supreme Court ruled Sioux Nation was entitled to $122.5 million in compensation for the US government seizure of the Black Hills in 1877, 1980; Cancer.

☿℞ Matt Urban awarded the Congressional Medal of Honor 36 years after the letter recommending him was lost, 1980; Cancer.

☿℞ DIA report concluded South Africa detonated an Atlantic Ocean nuclear test in September, 1979; *Critical Mass* listed 2300 malfunctions in 68 US nuclear plants in 1979, 1980; Cancer.

☿℞ Great Britain announced nuclear missile submarine modernization, 1980; Cancer.

☿℞ Summer Olympic Games opened in Moscow; 65 countries boycott, 1980; Cancer.

☿℞ Largest anti-nuclear demonstration since the early 60s in London; 50,000 marched for disarmament, 1980; Scorpio.

☿℞ Senate Armed Services Committee reported 147 false indications of USSR missile attacks on the US in previous 18 months, 1980; Scorpio.

☿℞ Ronald Reagan elected President; Republicans control US Senate for second time in 50 years, 1980; Scorpio.

☿℞ Former FBI agents found guilty of 1972–1973 civil rights violations, 1980; Scorpio.

☿℞ General Electric convicted in NJ of 1974 government bribes of $1 million, 1981; Pisces.

☿℞ East Germany said reunification is possible, switching ten-year position, 1981; Pisces.

☿℞ President Reagan's Energy Department discarded Carter's energy conservation program and delayed the imposition of home appliance energy efficiency standards, 1981; Aquarius.

☿℞ Center for Democratic Policy announced task force, new direction for the Democratic Party, 1981; Aquarius.

☿℞ Israeli air strike against Iraqi nuclear reactor, 1981; Cancer (SR).

☿℞ First mid-season strike by major league baseball players, 1981; Cancer.

☿℞ 17 Canadian Mounties charged with illegal police activities in early 70s, 1981; Cancer.

☿℞ US announced decision to sell weapons to China, a major policy reversal, 1981; Cancer.

☿℞ Swiss voters approved ERA amendment to Swiss Constitution, 1981; Cancer.

☿℞ First successful gene splicing to create a vaccine for animals or humans, 1981; Cancer.

☿℞ $93 million award against Johnson & Johnson for suppressing competition's electrical device for pain treatment, 1981; Gemini.

☿℞ Anwar El-Sadat, President of Egypt, assassinated, 1981; Scorpio (SR).

☿℞ *Washington Post* ran a story that ex-President Carter bugged President-elect Reagan in the Blair House before inauguration; then ran a front page retraction 18 days later, 1981; Scorpio (SR).

☿℞ Canadian Parliament urged federal action to deal with acid rain, 1981; Scorpio.

☿℞ Reagan lifted Carter 1977 ban on commercial reprocessing of nuclear fuel, 1981; Scorpio.

☿℞ Over 650,000 demonstrated in Bonn, Paris, Brussels, London, Rome, opposing NATO European nuclear weapons deployment, 1981; Scorpio.

☿℞ Amnesty International charged FBI misconduct with leaders of minority groups, 1981; Scorpio/Libra.

☿℞ Reagan said in the event of a limited nuclear war in Europe, the US may not escalate it to total annihilation, 1981; Libra.

☿℞ NRC announced engineering miscalculation, said Diablo Canyon nuclear reactor could collapse in an earthquake, 1981; Libra (SD).

☿℞ Soviet submarine ran aground in Swedish territorial waters; discovered by fishermen before they could get away, 1981; Libra (SD).

☿℞ CBS News reported US intelligence agencies suppressed and altered enemy troop estimates in the Vietnam War, 1982; Aquarius (SR).

☿℞ Ginna nuclear plant emergency, the worst since Three Mile Island, 1982; Aquarius.

☿℞ *Philadelphia Bulletin* ceased publication after 134 years, 1982; Aquarius.

☿℞ Alexander Haig threatened combat troop deployment in El Salvador, 1982; Aquarius.

☿℞ NRC recorded 1/3 of nation's nuclear plants were shut down for major and minor problems and maintenance, 1982; Aquarius.

☿℞ VP George Bush sought tax change favorable to drug industry, then broke off his involvement because of conflict of interest, 1982; Gemini (SR).

☿℞ President Reagan proposed changes in Clean Water Act that eliminated standards for industrial waste discharges, 1982; Gemini.

☿℞ Pentagon, Secretary of Defense Caspar Weinberger ordered preparation for nuclear counterattacks against USSR, 1982; Gemini.

☿℞ Pope John Paul II went to Canterbury, ending 450-year feud with Anglican Church; first Pope to set foot in England, 1982; Gemini.

☿℞ Israel invaded Lebanon, 1982; Gemini.

☿℞ National assessment of water found unsafe conditions for 63 percent of people in rural areas in the US, 1982; Gemini.

☿℞ Four-million-year-old bones found in Ethiopia, 1982; Gemini.

☿℞ 750,000 marched in NYC for nuclear disarmament, 1982; Gemini (SD).

☿℞ Argentina surrendered to Great Britain in Falklands War, 1982; Gemini (SD).

☿℞ First regular season strike in the 63-year history of the NFL, 1982; Libra.

☿℞ El Salvador ruled that indictments against National Guardsmen who killed four nuns were defective; ordered the court to begin indictment procedures again, 1983; Aquarius.

☿℞ Appeals Court struck down $1.8 billion MCI award against AT&T; ordered a new trial upholding 8 or 10 findings against AT&T, 1983; Aquarius/Capricorn.

☿℞ TVA Browns Ferry nuclear plant radioactive water leak, 1983; Capricorn.

☿ᵣ US medical and political fact-finding mission found widespread torture and starvation in El Salvador; President Reagan insisted they were making human rights progress, 1983; Capricorn.

☿ᵣ Nuclear Regulatory Commission reported substandard steel used in building nuclear reactors since 1960, 1983; Capricorn.

☿ᵣ Nazi war criminal Klaus Barbie arrested in Bolivia, 1983; Capricorn (SD).

☿ᵣ Three Mile Island financial settlement payouts, 1983; Capricorn (SD).

☿ᵣ Huge Fresno, CA, earthquake injured 47, caused $31 million damage; worst in US since 1971, 1983; Taurus (SR).

☿ᵣ First successful fertilized frozen egg pregnancy in Australia, 1983; Taurus (SR).

☿ᵣ After four years of court challenges, hearings, and delays, concept artist Christo began to surround Biscayne Bay islets with pink plastic tarpaulins, 1983; Taurus.

☿ᵣ American Motors announced joint venture with China; first US carmaker to enter Chinese market, 1983; Taurus.

☿ᵣ Largest terrorist bomb attack in South African history, 18 killed, over 200 injured, 1983; Taurus.

☿ᵣ Over 35,000 marched in Argentina's largest-ever human rights protest, 1983; Taurus.

☿ᵣ US announced it would ease restrictions on sale of sensitive hi-tech items to China, 1983; Taurus (SD).

☿ᵣ One million women took part in 600 events across Great Britain and Ireland for the International Women's Day for Disarmament, 1983; Taurus (SD).

☿ᵣ South Korean jetliner 007 shot down by Soviets, 269 killed, 1983; Libra (SR).

☿ᵣ First use of US naval firepower in the Mediterranean since WW II, 1983; Libra/Virgo.

☿ᵣ US Federal judge ruled unconstitutional the US government's attempt to restrict three Canadian films, including one anti-nuclear film which had won an Academy Award April 1983, 1983; Libra/Virgo.

☿R Albert Einstein's FBI file released; he had been investigated for: heading a spy ring; a Communist plot to take over Hollywood; participating in the Lindbergh kidnapping; inventing a death ray and a robot capable of reading human minds, 1983; Virgo.

☿R St. Kitts-Nevis, Britain's oldest Caribbean colony, gained independence, 1983; Virgo.

☿R Marc Rich and Co. indicted in largest commodities-trading tax evasion case in US history, 1983; Virgo.

☿R Two week US cold wave caused over 400 deaths, $250–350 million in citrus damage, 1983; Capricorn (SR).

☿R US Energy Dep't announced no nuclear dump site recommendation until Dec. 90, three years after 1987 Congressional deadline established by the Nuclear Waste Policy of 1982, 1983; Capricorn.

☿R US withdrew from UNESCO, 1983; Capricorn.

☿R AT&T divestiture of Bell System local companies into seven regionals, 1984; Capricorn.

☿R Australian woman gave birth to first lab-conceived quadruplets, 1984; Capricorn.

☿R Benazir Bhutto released after two years in a Pakistani prison, 1984; Capricorn (SD).

☿R Reagan's Task Force on Food Assistance concluded that undernutrition was not a problem in the US; the report was immediately condemned by 42 national religious and anti-poverty groups, 1984; Capricorn (SD).

☿R 250,000 Australians marched for peace and disarmament on Palm Sunday, 1984; Taurus.

☿R CDC announced French isolation of virus thought to cause AIDS, 1984; Taurus.

☿R Great Britain said it would give up its administrative role in Hong Kong in 1997, 1984; Taurus.

☿R NY signed law to curb acid rain, the first in the US, 1984; Virgo (SR).

☿R US Navy recalled twelve Trident 1 nuclear missiles due to engine problems, 1984; Virgo (SR).

☿℞ Chief Justice Warren Burger refused to allow Diablo Canyon nuclear plant to begin full power operations, 1984; Virgo.

☿℞ Reagan announced a schoolteacher was to be chosen as the first "citizen passenger" to ride the space shuttle, 1984; Virgo.

☿℞ Typhoon Ike, worst Philippines storm in 20th century, killed 1400, injured 300, 500 missing, 1 million homeless, 1984; Virgo.

☿℞ Overnight trading began between Chicago and Singapore; first overnight link between US and a foreign exchange, 1984; Virgo (SD).

☿℞ Union Carbide pesticide gas leak disaster in Bhopal, India killed 1600, injured more than 50,000, 1984; Capricorn (SR).

☿℞ 138 countries and 21 international organizations signed the UN Convention on the Law of the Sea; US, Great Britain, West Germany refused to sign, 1984; Sagittarius.

☿℞ University of Arizona astronomers discovered first planet outside our solar system, orbiting 21 light years from Earth, 1984; Sagittarius.

☿℞ Two 7000 year-old human skulls found in Florida with brains largely intact, 1984; Sagittarius.

☿℞ Newspaper reports 1982–1983 Central American US combat missions killed 17; Pentagon denied report, 1984; Sagittarius.

☿℞ Great Britain, China signed accord granting Chinese sovereignty over Hong Kong in 1997, 1984; Sagittarius.

☿℞ Discovery of 33 organ chorale preludes by J. S. Bach, overlooked for 120 years, 1984; Sagittarius.

☿℞ Australia became first country to introduce an AIDS screening test program, 1985; Aries (SR).

☿℞ Pentagon barred GE from obtaining new contracts pending outcome of fraud charges; first such action taken against a major defense contractor (ban lifted 3 weeks later), 1985; Aries.

☿℞ EPA ordered sewage dumping by NYC moved farther out to sea because the present site 12 miles offshore was contaminating beaches in NJ and Long Island and endangering fish and shellfish, 1985; Aries.

☿℞ Japan notified US it would end all commercial whaling by March 1988, 1985; Aries.

☿℞ Dioxin-contaminated city of Times Beach, MO, was closed down and voted out of existence, 1985; Aries.

☿℞ Reagan announced plans for wreath-laying ceremony at Bitburg cemetery, where SS and German troops are buried; was assailed by Jewish groups and US veterans organizations; Reagan compounded the problem by calling German soldiers victims "just as surely as the victims in the concentration camps," 1985; Aries.

☿℞ USSR indicated willingness to suspend testing nuclear weapons, 1985; Aries (SD).

☿℞ EPA ordered by US federal judge to curb acid rain air pollution crossing into Canada, 1985; Leo (SR).

☿℞ Peru's first peaceful transfer of power to an elected president in forty years, 1985; Leo (SR).

☿℞ USSR announced nuclear test moratorium, 1985; Leo (SR).

☿℞ US Defense Secretary Weinberger claimed amidst Pentagon denials that the Salvadorian army had retaliated against those who killed six US citizens in June, 1985; Leo.

☿℞ NBC, CBS, ABC refused to air PSA's on behalf of teenage birth control, 1985; Leo.

☿℞ Montgomery Ward announced the end of its 113-year catalog operation, 1985; Leo.

☿℞ Delta airline jumbo jet crash at D/FW airport killed 137, 1985; Leo.

☿℞ Australia, New Zealand, six other nations declared the South Pacific a nuclear-free zone, 1985; Leo.

☿℞ Two Soviet astronauts revived a frozen derelict space station, 1985; Leo.

☿℞ Japan Airlines crash killed 520, worst single place disaster in history, 1985; Leo.

☿℞ Union Carbide toxic pesticide gas leak in West Virginia injured six, sent 134 to hospital, 1985; Leo.

☿℞ Navy lifted ban on new contracts with General Dynamics imposed for misconduct, 1985; Leo.

☿℞ Martial law ended in most of Turkey, seven years after it was declared, 1985; Sagittarius (SR).

☿℞ Pennzoil awarded $10.53 billion in suit against Texaco, 1985; Sagittarius (SR).

☿℞ John Pollard arrested for selling military secrets to Israel, Pakistan, 1985; Sagittarius.

☿℞ Discovery of previously unknown Shakespeare poem at Oxford, 1985; Sagittarius.

☿℞ Bloodiest airport hijacking in history in Malta; 60 killed, 1985; Sagittarius.

☿℞ Corazon Aquino announced her intent to challenge Marcos as a result of government whitewash and acquittal of the murderers of her husband, 1985; Sagittarius.

☿℞ An LA grand jury indicted General Dynamics on conspiring to defraud US Army, 1985; Sagittarius.

☿℞ EPA sued by seven states for violating Clean Air Act, endangering public health and causing environmental damage, 1985; Sagittarius/Scorpio.

☿℞ Australian scientists announced contraceptive bullet to reduce kangaroo population, replacing culling, 1986; Aries (SR).

☿℞ Supreme Court approved police deceit to prevent attorneys from seeing their clients, 1986; Aries/Pisces.

☿℞ Georgia parole board pardoned Leo Frank, dead since 1915, 1986; Aries/Pisces.

☿℞ FHA notified 65,000 farmers to renegotiate their loans or face foreclosure, 1986; Aries/Pisces.

☿℞ Soviet leader Gorbachev announced indefinite continuation of nuclear test moratorium, 1986; Aries/Pisces.

☿℞ Marcos documents seized, revealing global financial web

of money stolen from the Philippines; Swiss for first time ever freeze bank accounts, 1986; Pisces.

☿℞ Nat'l Academy of Sciences acid rain report conclusively links burning fuels with killing nature; was the central issue of Canadian/US summit meeting, 1986; Pisces.

☿℞ White House agreed to renovate homeless shelter after two years of wrangling with Mitch Snyder, 1986; Pisces.

☿℞ Smith-Kline recalled nonprescription capsule products after discovering rat poison contamination, 1986; Pisces.

☿℞ US conducted underground nuclear tests, 1986; Pisces.

☿℞ US warplanes attacked Libyan mainland; Reagan and Qaddafi both proclaimed victory, 1986; Pisces (SD).

☿℞ US nuclear weapons overseas storage places inadvertently identified, 1986; Leo (SR).

☿℞ Titanic wreckage viewed for the first time since 1912 sinking, 1986; Leo.

☿℞ Indiana court gave 14 year-old AIDS patient Ryan White the right to go to school, 1986; Leo.

☿℞ Tax reform group released a study claiming 42 large, profitable US corporations paid no taxes 1982–1985, 1986; Leo.

☿℞ Gorbachev extended nuclear test moratorium, 1986; Leo.

☿℞ Public report released that 2/3 of underground waste dumps in Ontario, Canada, pose a threat to human health, 1986; Leo.

☿℞ NIH experts said most pain sufferers were either over or under-medicated, 1986; Leo.

☿℞ Ontario government found half the companies surveyed dumped toxic chemicals in the Great Lakes in 1984, violating laws, 1986; Cancer.

☿℞ First Chinese factory bankruptcy since 1949 revolution, 1986; Cancer (SD).

☿℞ US Football League called off its 1986 season because of token damage award versus the NFL, 1986; Cancer (SD).

☿℞ Chemical spills polluted Rhine River in major environmental disaster, 1986; Scorpio (SR).

☿℞ National Academy of Sciences reported passive smoking health risk, 1986; Scorpio.

☿℞ John Walker sentenced to life in prison for spying against US, 1986; Scorpio.

☿℞ White House acknowledged for the first time the CIA's covert role in the Iranian arms for hostages swap, 1986; Scorpio.

☿℞ USSR announced withdrawal of nuclear missiles from near Finland and preparations to withdraw ballistic missile submarines from the Baltic Sea, 1986; Scorpio.

☿℞ Stolen government tax files on 16 million Canadians recovered, 1986; Scorpio.

☿℞ *Washington Post* reported seven-year CIA covert activity in Iran; Sam Nunn found seven major contradictions in Reagan's comments, 1986; Scorpio.

☿℞ EPA issued final "bubble policy" rules on air pollution allowances, 1986; Scorpio.

☿℞ British scientists confirmed "greenhouse effect" for the first time, 1986; Scorpio (SD).

☿℞ Mt. Mihara in Japan erupted, first in 39 years, worst in two centuries, 1986; Scorpio (SD).

☿℞ Chilean astronomer discovered massive supernova 160,000 light years from Earth, 1987; Pisces.

☿℞ USSR ended nuclear moratorium with Kazakhstan underground tests, 1987; Pisces.

☿℞ Pakistan announced the development of a nuclear bomb, then disavowed the report, 1987; Pisces.

☿℞ John Pollard sentenced to life in prison for spying for Israel, 1987; Pisces.

☿℞ Mobile, Alabama banned 40 high school textbooks for promoting the "religion" of "secular humanism," 1987; Pisces.

☿℞ 7.3 earthquake in Ecuador killed over 300, halted oil industry; 4000 missing, 20,000 homeless, 1987; Pisces.

☿℞ US Supreme Court affirmed police may conduct warrantless searches, 1987; Cancer.

☿℞ Justice Lewis Powell retired from Supreme Court; Robert Bork nominated, 1987; Cancer.

☿℞ Nazi Klaus Barbie found guilty of crimes against humanity in France, got life in prison, 1987; Cancer.

☿℞ Oliver North implicated Schultz, Abrams, Casey, and Reagan in Congressional deception, 1987; Cancer.

☿℞ Marcos plot to return to power in Philippines publicly revealed, 1987; Cancer.

☿℞ US House banned cigarette smoking on air flights of two hours or less, 1987; Cancer (SD).

☿℞ Taiwan lifted martial law after 48 years, 1987; Cancer (SD).

☿℞ Dow Jones Industrial Average dropped 508 points in one day, over 600 over four days; triggered worldwide stock market crashes, 1987; Scorpio (SR).

☿℞ US oil tanker in Kuwait hit by Iranian missile; US bombed Iranian oil rig, announced embargo, 1987; Scorpio (SR).

☿℞ Illinois jury fined Monsanto $16.2 Million for 1979 toxic chemical spill, 1987; Scorpio.

☿℞ US Senate rejected Robert Bork for Supreme Court, 1987; Scorpio.

☿℞ Canada approved agreement giving Quebec special status, 1987; Scorpio.

☿℞ EPA ordered asbestos removal from public schools, 1987; Scorpio.

☿℞ US Senate approved smoking ban on flights 90 minutes or less, 1987; Scorpio.

☿℞ Reagan nominated Douglas Ginsburg for Supreme Court; Ginsburg withdrew nine days later, 1987; Scorpio/Libra.

☿℞ *Wall St. Journal* reported that cervical cancer pap smear fails about 25 percent of the time, 1987; Libra.

☿℞ US warship fired on suspected Iranian gunboat, later revealed as an unarmed Arab fishing boat, 1987; Libra.

☿℞ First female elected to head Nat'l Council of Churches, 1987; Libra (SD).

☿℞ Senate ratified pact to ban ocean dumping of plastics, 1987; Libra (SD).

☿℞ FBI defended surveillance against hundreds of US citizens opposed to Reagan's Central America policy, 1988; Aquarius (SR).

☿℞ Supreme Court announced surrogate motherhood contracts illegal, 1988; Aquarius.

☿℞ International historians found that Kurt Waldheim knew of war atrocities, 1988; Aquarius.

☿℞ Delaware, Florida, Georgia, Missouri, Oklahoma, and Virginia found in noncompliance with 1964 law banning segregation in colleges and universities, 1988; Aquarius.

☿℞ Soviet Academy of Sciences main library caught fire; 400,000 books destroyed, more than 3 million damaged, 1988; Aquarius.

☿℞ Georgia Tech shut down its nuclear reactor because of contamination spread; US Energy Department said it would not reopen its plutonium producing reactor at Hanford, 1988; Aquarius.

☿℞ French and Israeli scientists demonstrated that modern humans lived 92,000 years ago, more than doubling previous estimates, 1988; Aquarius.

☿℞ Televangelist Jimmy Swaggart confessed his "sin" to more than 6000, 1988; Aquarius (SD).

☿℞ Australian customs found 12 tons of weapons bound for Fiji uprising, 1988; Gemini (SR).

☿℞ California acid pits cleanup agreement reached; W. R. Grace and Co. pleaded guilty to lying to EPA about toxic chemicals in Massachusetts; Monsanto agreed to $1.5 million settlement in West Virginia chemical poisoning, 1988; Gemini.

☿℞ After six years of negotiation, Antarctica was opened to commercial mining, 1988; Gemini.

☿℞ South African massive three-day, 2 million worker strike, 1988; Gemini.

☿℞ NJ jury found a tobacco company liable in the death of a

smoker; first such ruling in over 300 lawsuits, 1988; Gemini.

☿℞ Kremlin admitted Stalin unjustly deported 31,000 Latvians to Siberia and other remote places between 1940–1949, 1988; Gemini.

☿℞ Massive Pentagon defense contractor fraud/bribery scandal revealed, 1988; Gemini.

☿℞ NASA confirmed the greenhouse effect, 1988; Gemini (SD).

☿℞ Florida school district agreed to pay $1.1 million to family whose AIDS-infected sons were denied schooling, 1988; Libra (SR).

☿℞ Space shuttle Discovery launched, first since Challenger disaster, 1988; Libra (SR).

☿℞ US Congress revised US welfare system for first time since 1935, 1988; Libra.

☿℞ FBI found guilty of discriminating against Hispanics, 1988; Libra.

☿℞ Civil Rights Act of 1964 extended to House of Representatives staff, 1988; Libra.

☿℞ EPA announced it would allow new cancer-causing pesticides to replace older cancer-causing pesticides, 1988; Libra.

☿℞ Archbishop of Turin announced testing of the Shroud of Turin dates it at A.D. 1280, 1988; Libra.

☿℞ Great Britain banned TV and radio broadcasts by 11 North Ireland organizations, including Sinn Fein, 1988; Libra (SD).

☿℞ Congress passed a bill restricting commercials broadcast to children; made genocide a crime, putting into effect a 1948 UN treaty signed by Truman, 1988; Libra (SD).

☿℞ On MLK's birthday, President-elect George Bush "pledges his administration will pursue equality for black Americans; the predominantly black Overton section of Miami erupts into rioting after a black motorcyclist is killed by an Hispanic police officer," 1989; Aquarius (SR).

☿℞ Reagan pardoned George Steinbrenner's 1974 conviction for illegal Nixon donations two days before leaving office, 1989; Aquarius.

☿℞ *NY Times* reported Iran used US, West Germany, others to illegally import poison gas chemicals, 1989; Aquarius/Capricorn.

☿℞ Argentine ship ran aground in Antarctica, spilling diesel fuel; wildlife threatened, passengers and crew safe, 1989; Aquarius/Capricorn.

☿℞ 25,000 Stalin purge victims rehabilitated when Central Committee passed mass conviction reversal, 1989; Aquarius/Capricorn.

☿℞ A. Stroessner, Paraguay's President/Dictator for 34 years, overthrown in coup, 1989; Capricorn.

☿℞ Shevardnadze became first Soviet Foreign Minister in thirty years to visit China, 1989; Capricorn.

☿℞ President Bush unveiled $126 billion S&L bailout plan, 1989; Capricorn (SD).

☿℞ VP Dan Quayle mangled UNCF slogan, saying "What a waste it is to lose one's mind, or not to have a mind. How true that is," 1989; Gemini (SR).

☿℞ US Federal court ordered the VA to broaden Agent Orange health problem criteria, 1989; Gemini (SR).

☿℞ US, Kenya, called for worldwide ban on the ivory trade, 1989; Gemini (SR).

☿℞ Bush administration reversed itself, said it would work to curb global warming, 1989; Gemini (SR).

☿℞ 1000 students began a hunger strike in China over political reforms; within days over one million people demonstrated for democracy, and hundreds of thousands of students and workers defied martial law, 1989; Gemini (SR).

☿℞ US, Washington state agreed to clean up Hanford nuclear dump over a 30-year period, 1989; Gemini (SR).

☿℞ China revealed it sent 300,000 troops to Vietnam to fight US after denying it for decades, 1989; Gemini.

☿℞ Denver approved new $2.3 billion airport to replace Stapleton, 1989; Gemini.

☿℞ USSR gas pipeline explosion engulfed two trains, killing 190, 720 hospitalized, 270 missing, 1989; Taurus (SD).

☿℞ Sri Lankan floods, mudslides killed over 300, left 100,000 homeless, 1989; Taurus (SD).

☿℞ Ayatollah Khomeini died; eight die, hundreds injured in body-viewing, 1989; Taurus (SD).

☿℞ Hundreds ruthlessly killed when Chinese troops stormed Tian An Men Square to crush the pro-democracy movement, 1989; Taurus (SD).

☿℞ Largest exodus of East Germans to the west since the Berlin Wall was built in 1961, 1989; Libra (SR).

☿℞ 225,000 public service employees strike in Quebec, 1989; Libra.

☿℞ US Senate banned smoking on all domestic flights, 1989; Libra.

☿℞ French jetliner flying to Paris exploded from a bomb, killing 171; 1989; Libra.

☿℞ Anti-AIDS drug tricosanthin study released showing "promising results," 1989; Libra.

☿℞ Vietnam withdrew troops from Cambodia after over ten years of war, 1989; Libra/Virgo.

☿℞ President Bush signed funding for never-completed Texas supercollider, 1989; Virgo.

☿℞ Panama took control over the Panama Canal, 1990; Capricorn (SR).

☿℞ 9000 gallons of PCB contaminated oil spilled into St. Lawrence River (not discovered for a week), 1990; Capricorn (SR).

☿℞ 10,000 gallons of gasoline dumped in Monongahela River, 1990; Capricorn (SR).

☿℞ 567,000 gallon Exxon oil pipeline leak in NY harbor, 1990; Capricorn.

☿℞ Worst Pakistani rail disaster killed 210, injures 700, 1990; Capricorn.

☿ᴿ Appeals court overturned 1988 verdict against Liggett tobacco company, but reinstated claims, 1990; Capricorn.

☿ᴿ Iraq offered to make peace with Iran, 1990; Capricorn.

☿ᴿ China lifted martial law after eight months, 1990; Capricorn.

☿ᴿ AT&T sued MCI over "slamming" practices, 1990; Capricorn.

☿ᴿ Spain launched a campaign to encourage men to do more domestic chores, 1990; Capricorn.

☿ᴿ Amnesty International released Saudi torture report; Saudis denied they torture or have political prisoners, 1990; Capricorn.

☿ᴿ The "Great Attractor" gravitational source 150 million light years away announced, confirmed "continental" galaxy/cluster theory, 1990; Capricorn.

☿ᴿ AT&T nationwide phone operations disrupted for nine hours, 1990; Capricorn.

☿ᴿ Thousands stormed East German secret police headquarters, 1990; Capricorn.

☿ᴿ RJR Tobacco canceled plans to market cigarettes aimed at black smokers, 1990; Capricorn (SD).

☿ᴿ Worst flooding in Australia in 100 years, 1990; Taurus (SR).

☿ᴿ Lebanese kidnappers released Reed, Polhill, after over three years, 1990; Taurus (SR).

☿ᴿ Earth Day 1990; 200 million participated in 140 nations, 1990; Taurus (SR).

☿ᴿ First visit of Chinese Premier to USSR in 26 years, 1990; Taurus (SR).

☿ᴿ Hubble space telescope went into orbit seven years after launch date, with immediate communications problems, 1990; Taurus.

☿ᴿ American College of Physicians called for nationalized health care, 1990; Taurus.

☿ᴿ 20,000 strike in Korean shipyard, did battle with 10,000 police, 1990; Taurus.

☿℞ Largest native land claim in Canadian history settled, gave 135,000 square miles and $520 million to Inuit tribe, 1990; Taurus.

☿℞ China lifted martial law in Tibet, 1990; Taurus.

☿℞ First formal talks between the ANC and the South African government, 1990; Taurus.

☿℞ US government approved AZT for AIDS, 1990; Taurus.

☿℞ Latvia and Estonia declared independence from USSR, 1990; Taurus.

☿℞ Florida execution went awry; sparks and flames shot out of dead man's head, 1990; Taurus.

☿℞ RTC lowered prices, dumped massive amounts of property in S&L bailout, 1990; Taurus.

☿℞ US opposed UN plan to reduce ozone globally, 1990; Taurus.

☿℞ 100,000 pro-democracy students and workers protested in South Korea, 1990; Taurus.

☿℞ Armenia declared independence from USSR; asserted control over Nagorno-Karabakh, 1990; Virgo (SR).

☿℞ Musical subliminal messages judged "not proved," legally, in teen suicides, 1990; Virgo (SR).

☿℞ East and West Germany signed reunification treaty, established Berlin as new capitol, 1990; Virgo.

☿℞ Amnesty International report on Brazilian death squads killing many hundreds of street children a year, torturing more, 1990; Virgo.

☿℞ Last major ivory-importing nation agreed to global ban on ivory trade, 1990; Virgo.

☿℞ Northern hemisphere ozone hole reported for first time, 1990; Virgo.

☿℞ NRC set lower radiation exposure limits for nuclear workers; first revisions in 30 years were based on 1977 recommendations, 1991; Capricorn (SR).

☿℞ Byron de la Beckwith charged for third time with killing Medgar Evars, 1991; Capricorn.

☿℞ Salman Rushdie publicly renounced his book *The Satanic*

Verses; Iran reaffirmed its death decree against him, 1991; Capricorn/Sagittarius.

☿ᵣ Iraq agreed to a formal cease-fire ending its Persian Gulf War with Iran; 2 million Kurds fled to Iran and Turkey, 1991; Aries (SR).

☿ᵣ Georgia declared independence from USSR, 1991; Aries.

☿ᵣ Worst Italian maritime disaster since WW II near Lavorno killed 140, spilled 150,000 barrels of oil creating 1.5 square mile slick; the next day, a supertanker explosion spilled 1 million barrels of oil off Genoa; slick was 12–30 square miles, 1991; Aries.

☿ᵣ Norway called off its annual whale hunt for first time since the 16th century, 1991; Aries.

☿ᵣ *Washington Post* reported China was helping Algeria build a nuclear weapons plant, 1991; Aries.

☿ᵣ 7.4 earthquake hit Costa Rica and region, worst since 1910 killed 95, injured 800, 1991; Aries.

☿ᵣ 70 tornadoes in TX, OK, AR, KS, MO, NE, IA killed 23, cause tens of millions in damages, 1991; Aries (SD).

☿ᵣ Hundreds of police battled pro-apartheid neo-Nazis trying to stop a speech, 1991; Virgo (SR).

☿ᵣ Chile's Hudson volcano erupted for first time in twenty years, 1991; Virgo (SR).

☿ᵣ Shiite Muslim kidnappers released hostages Tracy, Leyraud, 1991; Virgo.

☿ᵣ Baseball Hall of Fame hosted reunion of Negro League players, 1991; Virgo.

☿ᵣ Australian computer hacker charged with shutting down NASA and changing nuclear data at Livermore in 1990, 1991; Virgo.

☿ᵣ Coup by Soviet hard-liners against Gorbachev failed; Yeltsin led pro-democracy opposition, Gorbachev resigned as head of Communist Party, 1991; Virgo/Leo.

☿ᵣ Eight Soviet republics declared or re-affirmed transitional or complete independence: Lithuania, Estonia, Latvia, Armenia, Georgia, Ukraine, Byelorussia, Moldavia, 1991; Leo.

☿ᴿ Australia, Scandinavian nations, European Community recognized new Baltic nations, 1991; Leo.

☿ᴿ Communist 74-year reign of USSR ended, 1991; Leo (SD).

☿ᴿ New long jump record, erased track's longest-standing record (1968), 1991; Leo (SD).

☿ᴿ Judge awarded back pay to 67 female Navy employees in 18-year-old sex bias case, 1991; Sagittarius (SR).

☿ᴿ California dust storm created 93-car, 11-tractor-trailer, 4-mile-long pile-up killing 17, injuring more than 150, 1991; Sagittarius (SR).

☿ᴿ Ukraine voted itself formally independent from USSR; Commonwealth of Independent States formed and agreed to end the Soviet Union, 1991; Sagittarius.

☿ᴿ USAID suspended distribution of 50 million condoms to Egypt after finding they were being sold as toy balloons, 1991; Sagittarius.

☿ᴿ Final agreement with Inuit created 772,000 square mile new Canadian Territory, Nunavut, 1991; Sagittarius.

☿ᴿ White South African voters approved referendum to negotiate an end to white minority rule, 1992; Aries (SR).

☿ᴿ Iraq admitted it hid ballistic missiles, chemical weapons from UN inspectors, 1992; Aries.

☿ᴿ Arizona resumed executions after 29 years, 1992; Pisces.

☿ᴿ Natural Resources Defense Council reported that over 2000 US beaches were closed in 1991 because of raw sewage or other pollutants, 1992; Leo.

☿ᴿ Agreement by Czech and Slovak Republics to separate, 1992, Leo.

☿ᴿ Film of "Tailhook" sex abuse disclosed, 1992; Leo.

☿ᴿ Canadian study linked drinking cows milk with juvenile diabetes, 1992; Leo.

☿ᴿ Chinese airliner exploded, killing 106, injuring 26, 1992; Leo.

☿ᴿ Iraq reasserted sovereignty over Kuwait, 1992; Leo.

☿ᴿ Chinese stock market riots; more than one million people involved, 1992; Leo (SD).

☿R NAFTA draft announced after 14 months of negotiations, 1992; Leo (SD).

☿R First new EPA regulations in 18 years toughened worker pesticide exposure standards, 1992; Leo (SD).

☿R JAMA reported that nearly half of US coronary angiograms were unnecessary, 1992; Sagittarius (SR).

☿R Church of England voted to allow women to become priests, 1992; Sagittarius (SR).

☿R Superman died, 1992; Sagittarius.

☿R 45 tornadoes in eleven states killed 25, injured hundreds, caused $425 million in property damage, 1992; Sagittarius/Scorpio.

☿R Ernst & Young fined $400 million for faulty S&L audits costing US taxpayers $4.5 billion, 1992; Scorpio.

☿R FDA recommended folic acid during pregnancy to prevent spina bifida and incomplete brain development; recommended taxol from Pacific Northwest Yew tree as treatment for ovarian cancer, 1992; Scorpio.

☿R China's worst air disaster killed 141, 1992; Scorpio.

☿R Doctors for first time repaired brain damage using fetal tissue implants, 1992; Scorpio.

☿R World Trade Center bombing, 1993; Pisces (SR).

☿R ATF launched its raid on Branch Davidians in Waco, Texas, 1993; Pisces (SR).

☿R Florida became first state to make breastfeeding in public legal, 1993; Pisces.

☿R North Korea became first nation in history to withdraw from the Nuclear Non-proliferation Treaty; worldwide condemnation followed, 1993; Pisces.

☿R US Defense Secretary recommended closing 31 US military bases, cutbacks at 134 others; loss of 81,000 jobs estimated, 1993; Pisces.

☿R Biggest wave of criminal violence in the history of India; bombing killed over 300, injures 1100, 1993; Pisces.

☿R Blizzard hit US east coast; 109 mph winds spawned dozens of tornadoes, cut off power to 3 million homes, killed over 213, caused $800 million in damages, 1993; Pisces.

☿℞ "Motor Voter" bill passed US Congress, 1993; Pisces.

☿℞ Russia, US announced extension of nuclear test ban, 1993; Cancer (SR).

☿℞ Everglades restoration agreement announced after five years of legal battles over sugar industry pollution, 1993; Cancer.

☿℞ Japan's ruling political party (LDF) denied a majority for first time in 38 years, 1993; Cancer.

☿℞ Russia announced withdrawal of all old currency, gave people two weeks to convert to new, 1993; Cancer (SD).

☿℞ Former chief of East German secret police convicted of two 1931 murders, 1993; Scorpio (SR).

☿℞ 12 Southern California fires 200 miles long in six counties destroyed over 1000 homes, 200,000 acres; $500 million in damage, 1993; Scorpio (SR).

☿℞ Russia permitted the unrestricted sale, rental, leasing of land for the first time since 1917, 1993; Scorpio (SR).

☿℞ Smoking linked to lower estrogen levels, osteoporosis in women, 1994; Pisces (SR).

☿℞ NASA confirmed they were using "Superglue" to repair space shuttle engine pumps for six years (unauthorized), 1994; Pisces (SR).

☿℞ CIA spook A. Ames arrested for spying for USSR and Russia, 1994; Pisces/Aquarius.

☿℞ After 23 years, Supreme Court Justice Harry Blackmun reversed stance, denounced capital punishment as unconstitutional, 1994; Pisces/Aquarius.

☿℞ "Whitewater" inquiry began, 1994; Aquarius.

☿℞ West Bank massacre in Hebron by lone gunman killed 40, wounded 150; worst since 1967, 1994; Aquarius.

☿℞ Nicole Brown murdered; O. J. Simpson charged eight days later, 1994; Cancer (SR).

☿℞ Supreme Court overruled states and cities, said homeowners may post opinion signs on their own property, 1994; Cancer (SR).

☿℞ North Korean nuclear inspection crisis; ex-President Carter defused tensions, 1994; Cancer (SR).

☿℞ US Senate began "Whitewater" inquiry, 1994; Cancer (SR).

☿℞ $98 million settlement reached in Love Canal pollution suit after fourteen years, 1994; Cancer.

☿℞ PLO chairman Yasir Arafat ended 27-year exile, returned to Palestine, 1994; Cancer/Gemini.

☿℞ EPA announced review and phase-out of 36 cancer-causing pesticides and herbicides over 5 years, 1994; Scorpio.

☿℞ Houston, TX floods killed 19, forced 11,000 to evacuate; ruptured pipelines spilling 200,000 gallons of fuel, 1994; Scorpio/Libra.

☿℞ Jordan, Israel signed peace treaty formally ending 46-year war, 1994; Scorpio/Libra.

☿℞ FDA urged tests for up to 25,000 faulty wired pacemakers in US patients, 1995; Aquarius (SR).

☿℞ Opening arguments presented in O. J. Simpson murder trial, 1995; Aquarius (SR).

☿℞ Male and female brains found to function differently, 1995; Aquarius (SR) & (SD).

☿℞ CDC announced AIDS as leading cause of death in 1993 among all people in US aged 25–44, 1995; Aquarius.

☿℞ Neutrinos found to have mass for first time since 1956 discovery, 1995; Aquarius.

☿℞ IMF, US, BIS authorized $49.5 billion loan for Mexico, 1995; Aquarius.

☿℞ Dutch floods killed 40; 250,000 evacuated, $1.18 billion in damage, 1995; Aquarius.

☿℞ Scientists found the place in the brain that stores perfect pitch, 1995; Aquarius.

☿℞ Terrorists killed gypsies in Austria, using toy cars to stash bombs; thousands protested, 1995; Aquarius.

☿℞ Mastermind of World Trade Center bombing caught, 1995; Aquarius.

☿℞ US DOE announced 9000 were used as subjects in 154 Cold War radiation experiments, 1995; Aquarius.

☿℞ PRI dealt their biggest setback in Mexican elections in 66 years; Zapatistas installed alternative governor in Chiapas, 1995; Aquarius.

☿℞ Lloyd's of London announced major $25 billion debt restructuring, 1995; Gemini (SR).

☿℞ Bavarian government overturned court ruling making a beer garden close early after 20,000 protest, including government ministers, 1995; Gemini (SR).

☿℞ NATO bombed Bosnian Serb weapons depots for first time; Bosnian Serbs took hundreds as hostages, 1995; Gemini (SR).

☿℞ Major ebola virus outbreak reported in Zaire, 1995; Gemini (SR).

☿℞ Phillip Morris recalled 8 billion filter cigarettes for pesticide contamination, 1995; Gemini.

☿℞ 7.5 earthquake in Sakhalin, Russia, killed 2000, 1995; Gemini.

☿℞ Mojave Desert nuclear waste dump granted to California, 1995; Gemini.

☿℞ Studies released showing over 1/5 of US population drink contaminated tap water causing over 1000 deaths/year and more than 7 million illnesses, 1995; Gemini.

☿℞ Space shuttle Discovery liftoff delayed because of 135 holes created by mating woodpeckers (owl decoys used to drive them away), 1995; Gemini.

☿℞ South Africa abolished the death penalty, 1995; Gemini.

☿℞ France announced it would resume nuclear testing in the South Pacific, 1995; Gemini.

☿℞ AT&T announced it would split into three companies; largest corporate breakup in US history, 1995; Libra (SR).

☿℞ Scientists reported finding "Giganotosaurus carolinii," largest known carnivorous dinosaur, 1995; Libra (SR).

☿℞ Thousands flocked to Hindu temples after hearing that statues of Ganesh were drinking milk, 1995; Libra (SR).

☿℞ Both sides formally rested in O. J. murder trial; O. J. acquitted, 1995; Libra (SR).

☿℞ Jury convicted all ten suspects in World Trade Center bombing case, 1995; Libra (SR).

☿℞ 40,000 migrating birds killed by raw sewage spill in Mexico, 1995; Libra.

☿℞ CIA director announced major shakeup, firings over Guatemala operations lies and misconduct, 1995; Libra.

☿℞ France conducted underground South Pacific nuclear test, 1995; Libra.

☿℞ US federal restrictions lessened on sale of high performance computers to foreign countries, 1995; Libra.

☿℞ Amtrak derailment in Arizona due to sabotage killed one, injured 100, 1995; Libra.

☿℞ UN Center for Human Rights records on Croatian human rights violations stolen, 1996; Aquarius (SR).

☿℞ Chinese government restricted information flow into the country, 1996; Aquarius.

☿℞ Major League Baseball approved interleague play for the first time, 1996; Capricorn.

☿℞ La Fenice, 204-year-old Venetian opera house, destroyed by fire, 1996; Capricorn (SD).

☿℞ Medical breakthroughs announced: Sex unlikely to trigger heart attacks, treadmill is best machine for fat burning, location where post traumatic stress disorder is stored in the brain, and multiple births do better when they leave the womb earlier than previously assumed, 1996; Taurus.

☿℞ World's biggest ruby ($9\frac{1}{2}$ lb.) found in Burma, 1996; Taurus.

☿℞ The Congress Party, India's sole ruling party for fifty years, was ousted by the opposition, 1996; Taurus.

☿℞ News released that Cdr. Byrd never made it to the North Pole, 1996; Taurus.

☿℞ "Magic" Johnson officially retired from basketball for the third time, 1996; Taurus.

☿℞ Executive order signed by President Clinton revoking Vietnam as a war zone, 1996; Taurus.

☿℞ Tornado in Bangladesh flattened eighty villages in less than thrity minutes, killing over 500, injuring 33,000, 1996; Taurus.

☿℞ Largest banking error in history made 800 overnight multimillionaires, 1996; Taurus.

☿℞ An original "Raphael" found among thousands of old drawings in the Chicago Art Institute, 1996; Taurus.

☿℞ Marvin Hinton formally named as the man behind the "Piltdown Man" skull hoax, 1996; Taurus.

☿℞ Eight senior citizens busted for playing pinochle; charges dropped after a few days, 1996; Taurus.

☿℞ US launched missile strike against Iraq, 1996, Virgo (SR).

☿℞ Teachers in India undress, demanding extra pay, 1996. Virgo.

☿℞ Report released that Stalin's statue was torn down in Prague, replaced by one of Michael Jackson, 1996; Virgo.

☿℞ Hundreds of Spaniards panicked over reported alien invasion of NYC, 1996; Virgo.

☿℞ Scientific study said Edgar Allen Poe died in 1849 of rabies, not alcohol, 1996; Virgo.

☿℞ Typhoon Sally killed 114, destroyed 200,000 homes in China; hurricane Fran caused $1.2 billion in damage in US, 1996; Virgo.

☿℞ CIA web site broken into by Swedish hackers, 1996; Virgo.

☿℞ President Clinton signed nuclear test ban treaty, 1996; Virgo (SD).

☿℞ Cabbage patch dolls ate children's hair, 1996; Capricorn.

☿℞ Ebola virus outbreak in Gabon, 1996; Capricorn.

☿℞ Norwegian politician shouted down charging moose, 1996; Capricorn.

☿℞ Europe's longest freeze in a decade killed 230, 1997; Capricorn.

☿℞ Five million gallon oil spill in Sea of Japan, 1997; Capricorn.

☿℞ An armored truck overturned in Miami, "raining hundreds of thousands of dollars" from an overpass onto poor people, 1997; Capricorn.

☿℞ Grapes found to be a cancer preventative, 1997; Capricorn.

☿℞ Pilgrimage fire killed 343 in Mecca, 1997; Taurus (SR).

☿℞ Chinese troops reentered Hong Kong for first time since Great Britain began its rule, 1997; Taurus.

☿℞ Wallet pickpocketed 15 years before returned to owner in South Africa, 1997; Taurus.

☿℞ Robert Kennedy assassination evidence alleged to have been tainted, 1997; Taurus.

☿℞ Ashes of Gene Roddenberry, Timothy Leary, others, shot into orbit, 1997; Taurus.

☿℞ Radio wave measurements indicated the universe has directions; force scientists to reconsider basic tenets about the birth of the universe, the speed of light, and the Theory of Relativity, 1997; Taurus.

☿℞ Two Mexican restaurants created 3600 foot, 4000 pound burrito, 1997; Aries (SD).

APPENDIX: MERCURY RETROGRADE POSITIONS 1900-2035

The following table lists the Mercury retrograde periods from 1900 through 2035, based on the calculations given in the Solar Fire Software Ephemeris. The stationary points listed may vary depending on which ephemeris you are using. Also, in any attempt to be precise regarding beginning and end points there will be variations of as much as a day based on what time zone and time of day one is measuring from. The following are approximated for the time zones of the North and South American continents. If you are using this for the Eastern Hemisphere, add a day to what is listed, e.g., Mar 14, 1900 becomes Mar 15, 1900 (better yet, get your chart precisely calculated!). Where there is only the stationary retrograde sign listed, it indicates that Mercury also went stationary direct in that same sign.

YEAR	DATE	SIGN	YEAR	DATE	SIGN
1900	Mar 14 to Apr 6	SR Aries	1910	Jan 16 to Feb 6	SR Aquarius
		SD Pisces			SD Capricorn
	July 17 to Aug 10	SR Leo		May 12 to Jun 5	SR Gemini
	Nov 9 to Nov 29	SR Sagittarius			SD Taurus
		SD Scorpio		Sep 12 to Oct 4	SR Libra
1901	Feb 25 to Mar 19	SR Pisces			SD Virgo
	Jun 28 to July 22	SR Cancer		Dec 31 to Jan 20 1911	SR Capricorn
	Oct 23 to Nov 12	SR Scorpio	1911	Apr 23 to May 17	SR Taurus
1902	Feb 9 to Mar 2	SR Pisces		Aug 25 to Sep 17	SR Virgo
		SD Aquarius		Dec 15 to Jan 4 1912	SR Capricorn
	Jun 9 to July 4	SR Cancer			SD Sagittarius
		SD Gemini	1912	Apr 4 to Apr 27	SR Aries
	Oct 6 to Oct 27	SR Scorpio		Aug 7 to Aug 31	SR Virgo
		SD Libra			SD Leo
1903	Jan 23 to Feb 13	SR Aquarius		Nov 28 to Dec 17	SR Sagittarius
	May 22 to Jun 14	SR Gemini	1913	Mar 17 to Apr 9	SR Aries
	Sep 19 to Oct 11	SR Libra			SD Pisces
1904	Jan 7 to Jan 28	SR Aquarius		July 20 to Aug 13	SR Leo
		SD Capricorn		Nov 11 to Dec 1	SR Sagittarius
	May 1 to May 24	SR Taurus			SD Scorpio
	Sep 1 to Sep 23	SR Libra	1914	Feb 28 to Mar 22	SR Pisces
		SD Virgo		July 1 to July 26	SR Cancer
	Dec 21 to Jan 9 1905	SR Capricorn		Oct 26 to Nov 15	SR Scorpio
1905	Apr 11 to May 6	SR Taurus	1915	Feb 11 to Mar 5	SR Pisces
		SD Aries			SD Aquarius
	Aug 14 to Sep 7	SR Virgo		Jun 13 to July 7	SR Cancer
	Dec 5 to Dec 25	SR Capricorn		Oct 9 to Oct 30	SR Scorpio
		SD Sagittarius			SD Libra
1906	Mar 25 to Apr 17	SR Aries	1916	Jan 26 to Feb 16	SR Aquarius
	July 28 to Aug 21	SR Leo		May 23 to Jun 16	SR Gemini
	Nov 19 to Dec 9	SR Sagittarius		Sep 21 to Oct 13	SR Libra
		SD Scorpio	1917	Jan 9 to Jan 29	SR Aquarius
1907	Mar 8 to Mar 31	SR Aries			SD Capricorn
		SD Pisces		May 4 to May 28	SR Taurus
	July 9 to Aug 3	SR Leo		Sep 4 to Sep 26	SR Libra
		SD Cancer			SD Virgo
	Nov 2 to Nov 22	SR Scorpio		Dec 24 to Jan 13 1918	SR Capricorn
1908	Feb 19 to Mar 12	SR Pisces	1918	Apr 15 to May 8	SR Taurus
	Jun 20 to July 14	SR Cancer		Aug 17 to Sep 10	SR Virgo
	Oct 16 to Nov 5	SR Scorpio		Dec 7 to Dec 27	SR Capricorn
		SD Libra			SD Sagittarius
1909	Feb 1 to Feb 22	SR Aquarius	1919	Mar 28 to Apr 20	SR Aries
	Jun 1 to Jun 25	SR Gemini		July 31 to Aug 23	SR Leo
	Sep 29 to Oct 20	SR Libra		Nov 21 to Dec 11	SR Sagittarius

YEAR	DATE	SIGN
1920	Mar 9 to Apr 1	SR Aries
		SD Pisces
	July 12 to Aug 5	SR Leo
		SD Cancer
	Nov 4 to Nov 24	SR Sagittarius
		SD Scorpio
1921	Feb 20 to Mar 15	SR Pisces
	Jun 23 to July 17	SR Cancer
	Oct 18 to Nov 8	SR Scorpio
1922	Feb 4 to Feb 25	SR Pisces
		SD Aquarius
	Jun 4 to Jun 28	SR Cancer
		SD Gemini
	Oct 2 to Oct 23	SR Scorpio
		SD Libra
1923	Jan 19 to Feb 8	SR Aquarius
		SD Capricorn
	May 16 to Jun 9	SR Gemini
	Sep 14 to Oct 7	SR Libra
		SD Virgo
1924	Jan 3 to Jan 23	SR Capricorn
	Apr 25 to May 19	SR Taurus
	Aug 27 to Sep 19	SR Virgo
	Dec 16 to Jan 5 1925	SR Capricorn
		SD Sagittarius
1925	Apr 7 to Apr 30	SR Taurus
		SD Aries
	Aug 10 to Sep 2	SR Virgo
		SD Leo
	Nov 30 to Dec 20	SR Sagittarius
1926	Mar 20 to Apr 12	SR Aries
	July 23 to Aug 16	SR Leo
	Nov 14 to Dec 3	SR Sagittarius
		SD Scorpio
1927	Mar 3 to Mar 25	SR Pisces
	July 4 to July 29	SR Leo
		SD Cancer
	Oct 28 to Nov 18	SR Scorpio
1928	Feb 14 to Mar 7	SR Pisces
		SD Aquarius
	Jun 15 to July 9	SR Cancer
	Oct 11 to Nov 1	SR Scorpio
		SD Libra
1929	Jan 28 to Feb 18	SR Aquarius
	May 26 to Jun 20	SR Gemini
	Sep 24 to Oct 16	SR Libra

YEAR	DATE	SIGN
1930	Jan 11 to Feb 1	SR Aquarius
		SD Capricorn
	May 7 to May 31	SR Gemini
		SD Taurus
	Sep 7 to Sep 29	SR Libra
		SD Virgo
	Dec 26 to Jan 15 1931	SR Capricorn
1931	Apr 18 to May 12	SR Taurus
	Aug 20 to Sep 13	SR Virgo
	Dec 10 to Dec 30	SR Capricorn
		SD Sagittarius
1932	Mar 30 to Apr 22	SR Aries
	Aug 2 to Aug 26	SR Virgo
		SD Leo
	Nov 23 to Dec 13	SR Sagittarius
1933	Mar 12 to Apr 4	SR Aries
		SD Pisces
	July 15 to Aug 8	SR Leo
	Nov 7 to Nov 27	SR Sagittarius
		SD Scorpio
1934	Feb 23 to Mar 18	SR Pisces
	Jun 26 to July 21	SR Cancer
	Oct 21 to Nov 11	SR Scorpio
1935	Feb 7 to Feb 28	SR Pisces
		SD Aquarius
	Jun 7 to July 1	SR Cancer
		SD Gemini
	Oct 4 to Oct 25	SR Scorpio
		SD Libra
1936	Jan 21 to Feb 11	SR Aquarius
	May 18 to Jun 11	SR Gemini
	Sep 16 to Oct 8	SR Libra
1937	Jan 4 to Jan 25	SR Aquarius
		SD Capricorn
	Apr 29 to May 22	SR Taurus
	Aug 30 to Sep 22	SR Virgo
	Dec 19 to Jan 8 1938	SR Capricorn
		SD Sagittarius
1938	Apr 10 to May 3	SR Taurus
		SD Aries
	Aug 13 to Sep 5	SR Virgo
		SD Leo
	Dec 3 to Dec 23	SR Sagittarius
1939	Mar 23 to Apr 15	SR Aries
	July 26 to Aug 19	SR Leo
	Nov 17 to Dec 7	SR Sagittarius
		SD Scorpio

YEAR	DATE	SIGN	YEAR	DATE	SIGN
1940	Mar 4 to Mar 27	SR Aries	1950	Jan 7 to Jan 28	SR Aquarius
		SD Pisces			SD Capricorn
	July 7 to July 31	SR Leo		May 2 to May 26	SR Taurus
		SD Cancer		Sep 3 to Sep 25	SR Libra
	Oct 30 to Nov 19	SR Scorpio			SD Virgo
1941	Feb 16 to Mar 10	SR Pisces		Dec 22 to Jan 11 1951	SR Capricorn
		SD Aquarius	1951	Apr 13 to May 7	SR Taurus
	Jun 18 to July 12	SR Cancer			SD Aries
	Oct 14 to Nov 4	SR Scorpio		Aug 16 to Sep 8	SR Virgo
		SD Libra		Dec 6 to Dec 26	SR Capricorn
1942	Jan 30 to Feb 21	SR Aquarius			SD Sagittarius
	May 30 to Jun 23	SR Gemini	1952	Mar 25 to Apr 18	SR Aries
	Sep 27 to Oct 18	SR Libra		July 28 to Aug 21	SR Leo
1943	Jan 14 to Feb 4	SR Aquarius		Nov 19 to Dec 9	SR Sagittarius
		SD Capricorn	1953	Mar 8 to Mar 31	SR Aries
	May 10 to Jun 3	SR Gemini			SD Pisces
		SD Taurus		July 10 to Aug 3	SR Leo
	Sep 10 to Oct 2	SR Libra			SD Cancer
		SD Virgo		Nov 3 to Nov 23	SR Sagittarius
	Dec 29 to Jan 18 1944	SR Capricorn			SD Scorpio
1944	Apr 20 to May 14	SR Taurus	1954	Feb 19 to Mar 13	SR Pisces
	Aug 22 to Sep 15	SR Virgo		Jun 22 to July 16	SR Cancer
	Dec 12 to Jan 1 1945	SR Capricorn		Oct 17 to Nov 7	SR Scorpio
		SD Sagittarius			SD Libra
1945	Apr 2 to Apr 25	SR Aries	1955	Feb 3 to Feb 24	SR Aquarius
	Aug 5 to Aug 29	SR Virgo		Jun 3 to Jun 27	SR Gemini
		SD Leo		Sep 30 to Oct 21	SR Libra
	Nov 26 to Dec 16	SR Sagittarius	1956	Jan 17 to Feb 7	SR Aquarius
1946	Mar 15 to Apr 7	SR Aries			SD Capricorn
		SD Pisces		May 13 to Jun 6	SR Gemini
	July 18 to Aug 11	SR Leo		Sep 12 to Oct 4	SR Libra
	Nov 9 to Nov 29	SR Sagittarius			SD Virgo
		SD Scorpio		Dec 31 to Jan 20 1957	SR Capricorn
1947	Feb 26 to Mar 21	SR Pisces	1957	Apr 24 to May 18	SR Taurus
	Jun 29 to July 24	SR Cancer		Aug 26 to Sep 18	SR Virgo
	Oct 24 to Nov 13	SR Scorpio		Dec 15 to Jan 4 1958	SR Capricorn
1948	Feb 9 to Mar 2	SR Pisces			SD Sagittarius
		SD Aquarius	1958	Apr 5 to Apr 29	SR Taurus
	Jun 10 to July 4	SR Cancer			SD Aries
		SD Gemini		Aug 8 to Sep 1	SR Virgo
	Oct 6 to Oct 27	SR Scorpio			SD Leo
		SD Libra		Nov 29 to Dec 19	SR Sagittarius
1949	Jan 23 to Feb 13	SR Aquarius	1959	Mar 18 to Apr 11	SR Aries
	May 21 to Jun 14	SR Gemini		July 21 to Aug 15	SR Leo
	Sep 19 to Oct 11	SR Libra		Nov 13 to Dec 3	SR Sagittarius
					SD Scorpio

YEAR	DATE	SIGN	YEAR	DATE	SIGN
1960	Feb 29 to Mar 23	SR Pisces	1970	Jan 3 to Jan 23	SR Capricorn
	July 2 to July 26	SR Leo		Apr 27 to May 21	SR Taurus
		SD Cancer		Aug 29 to Sep 21	SR Virgo
	Oct 26 to Nov 16	SR Scorpio		Dec 18 to Jan 7 1971	SR Capricorn
1961	Feb 12 to Mar 6	SR Pisces			SD Sagittarius
		SD Aquarius	1971	Apr 8 to May 2	SR Taurus
	Jun 13 to July 7	SR Cancer			SD Aries
	Oct 10 to Oct 30	SR Scorpio		Aug 11 to Sep 4	SR Virgo
		SD Libra			SD Leo
				Dec 2 to Dec 21	SR Sagittarius
1962	Jan 26 to Feb 16	SR Aquarius	1972	Mar 21 to Apr 13	SR Aries
	May 25 to Jun 18	SR Gemini		July 24 to Aug 17	SR Leo
	Sep 23 to Oct 14	SR Libra		Nov 15 to Dec 4	SR Sagittarius
1963	Jan 10 to Jan 31	SR Aquarius			SD Scorpio
		SD Capricorn	1973	Mar 3 to Mar 26	SR Pisces
	May 6 to May 29	SR Gemini		July 5 to July 30	SR Leo
		SD Taurus			SD Cancer
	Sep 6 to Sep 28	SR Libra		Oct 29 to Nov 18	SR Scorpio
		SD Virgo	1974	Feb 14 to Mar 9	SR Pisces
	Dec 25 to Jan 14 1964	SR Capricorn			SD Aquarius
1964	Apr 16 to May 9	SR Taurus		Jun 17 to July 11	SR Cancer
	Aug 18 to Sep 10	SR Virgo		Oct 12 to Nov 2	SR Scorpio
	Dec 8 to Dec 28	SR Capricorn			SD Libra
		SD Sagittarius	1975	Jan 29 to Feb 19	SR Aquarius
1965	Mar 28 to Apr 21	SR Aries		May 28 to Jun 21	SR Gemini
	Aug 1 to Aug 24	SR Virgo		Sep 26 to Oct 17	SR Libra
		SD Leo	1976	Jan 13 to Feb 3	SR Aquarius
	Nov 22 to Dec 12	SR Sagittarius			SD Capricorn
1966	Mar 11 to Apr 3	SR Aries		May 8 to Jun 1	SR Gemini
		SD Pisces			SD Taurus
	July 14 to Aug 7	SR Leo		Sep 8 to Sep 30	SR Libra
	Nov 5 to Nov 25	SR Sagittarius			SD Virgo
		SD Scorpio		Dec 27 to Jan 16 1977	SR Capricorn
1967	Feb 22 to Mar 16	SR Pisces	1977	Apr 19 to May 13	SR Taurus
	Jun 25 to July 19	SR Cancer		Aug 21 to Sep 13	SR Virgo
	Oct 20 to Nov 9	SR Scorpio		Dec 11 to Dec 31	SR Capricorn
1968	Feb 5 to Feb 27	SR Pisces			SD Sagittarius
		SD Aquarius	1978	Mar 31 to Apr 24	SR Aries
	Jun 5 to Jun 29	SR Cancer		Aug 4 to Aug 27	SR Virgo
		SD Gemini			SD Leo
	Oct 2 to Oct 23	SR Scorpio		Nov 25 to Dec 14	SR Sagittarius
		SD Libra	1979	Mar 14 to Apr 6	SR Aries
1969	Jan 19 to Feb 9	SR Aquarius			SD Pisces
	May 16 to Jun 9	SR Gemini		July 17 to Aug 10	SR Leo
	Sep 15 to Oct 7	SR Libra		Nov 8 to Nov 28	SR Sagittarius
		SD Virgo			SD Scorpio

YEAR	DATE	SIGN	YEAR	DATE	SIGN
1980	Feb 25 to Mar 18	SR Pisces	1990	Apr 22 to May 16	SR Taurus
	Jun 27 to July 21	SR Cancer		Aug 24 to Sep 16	SR Virgo
	Oct 22 to Nov 11	SR Scorpio		Dec 14 to Jan 2 1991	SR Capricorn
1981	Feb 7 to Mar 1	SR Pisces			SD Sagittarius
		SD Aquarius	1991	Apr 3 to Apr 27	SR Aries
	Jun 8 to July 2	SR Cancer		Aug 7 to Aug 30	SR Virgo
		SD Gemini			SD Leo
	Oct 5 to Oct 26	SR Scorpio		Nov 27 to Dec 17	SR Sagittarius
		SD Libra			
1982	Jan 22 to Feb 12	SR Aquarius	1992	Mar 16 to Apr 8	SR Aries
	May 20 to Jun 13	SR Gemini			SD Pisces
	Sep 18 to Oct 10	SR Libra		July 19 to Aug 12	SR Leo
1983	Jan 6 to Jan 26	SR Aquarius		Nov 10 to Nov 30	SR Sagittarius
		SD Capricorn			SD Scorpio
	Apr 30 to May 24	SR Taurus	1993	Feb 27 to Mar 21	SR Pisces
	Sep 1 to Sep 24	SR Libra		Jun 30 to July 25	SR Cancer
		SD Virgo		Oct 25 to Nov 14	SR Scorpio
	Dec 21 to Jan 10 1984	SR Capricorn	1994	Feb 10 to Mar 4	SR Pisces
1984	Apr 10 to May 4	SR Taurus			SD Aquarius
		SD Aries		Jun 11 to July 5	SR Cancer
	Aug 13 to Sep 6	SR Virgo			SD Gemini
	Dec 4 to Dec 23	SR Capricorn		Oct 8 to Oct 29	SR Scorpio
		SD Sagittarius			SD Libra
1985	Mar 23 to Apr 16	SR Aries	1995	Jan 25 to Feb 15	SR Aquarius
	July 27 to Aug 20	SR Leo		May 23 to Jun 16	SR Gemini
	Nov 17 to Dec 7	SR Sagittarius		Sep 21 to Oct 13	SR Libra
		SD Scorpio	1996	Jan 9 to Jan 29	SR Aquarius
1986	Mar 6 to Mar 29	SR Aries			SD Capricorn
		SD Pisces		May 3 to May 26	SR Taurus
	July 9 to Aug 2	SR Leo		Sep 3 to Sep 25	SR Libra
		SD Cancer			SD Virgo
	Nov 1 to Nov 21	SR Scorpio		Dec 23 to Jan 12 1997	SR Capricorn
1987	Feb 17 to Mar 12	SR Pisces	1997	Apr 14 to May 7	SR Taurus
		SD Aquarius			SD Aries
	Jun 20 to July 14	SR Cancer		Aug 17 to Sep 9	SR Virgo
	Oct 15 to Nov 5	SR Scorpio		Dec 6 to Dec 26	SR Capricorn
		SD Libra			SD Sagittarius
1988	Feb 1 to Feb 22	SR Aquarius	1998	Mar 26 to Apr 19	SR Aries
	May 31 to Jun 24	SR Gemini		July 30 to Aug 22	SR Leo
	Sep 28 to Oct 19	SR Libra		Nov 20 to Dec 10	SR Sagittarius
1989	Jan 15 to Feb 5	SR Aquarius	1999	Mar 9 to Apr 1	SR Aries
		SD Capricorn			SD Pisces
	May 11 to Jun 4	SR Gemini		July 12 to Aug 5	SR Leo
		SD Taurus			SD Cancer
	Sep 10 to Oct 3	SR Libra		Nov 4 to Nov 24	SR Sagittarius
		SD Virgo			SD Scorpio
	Dec 30 to Jan 19 1990	SR Capricorn			

YEAR	DATE	SIGN	YEAR	DATE	SIGN
2000	Feb 20 to Mar 14 Jun 22 to July 16 Oct 17 to Nov 7	SR Pisces SR Cancer SR Scorpio SD Libra	2010	Apr 17 to May 11 Aug 19 to Sep 12 Dec 9 to Dec 29	SR Taurus SR Virgo SR Capricorn SD Sagittarius
2001	Feb 3 to Feb 24 Jun 3 to Jun 27 Sep 30 to Oct 22	SR Pisces SD Aquarius SR Gemini SR Libra	2011	Mar 29 to Apr 22 Aug 2 to Aug 26 Nov 23 to Dec 13	SR Aries SR Virgo SD Leo SR Sagittarius
2002	Jan 18 to Feb 7 May 14 to Jun 7 Sep 13 to Oct 5	SR Aquarius SD Capricorn SR Gemini SR Libra SD Virgo	2012	Mar 11 to Apr 3 July 14 to Aug 7 Nov 6 to Nov 26	SR Aries SD Pisces SR Leo SR Sagittarius SD Scorpio
2003	Jan 1 to Jan 22 Apr 25 to May 19 Aug 27 to Sep 19 Dec 16 to Jan 5 2004	SR Capricorn SR Taurus SR Virgo SR Capricorn SD Sagittarius	2013	Feb 22 to Mar 16 Jun 25 to July 19 Oct 20 to Nov 9	SR Pisces SR Cancer SR Scorpio
2004	Apr 5 to Apr 29 Aug 9 to Sep 1 Nov 29 to Dec 19	SR Taurus SD Aries SR Virgo SD Leo SR Sagittarius	2014	Feb 6 to Feb 27 Jun 6 to Jun 30 Oct 3 to Oct 24	SR Pisces SD Aquarius SR Cancer SD Gemini SR Scorpio SD Libra
2005	Mar 19 to Apr 11 July 22 to Aug 15 Nov 13 to Dec 3	SR Aries SR Leo SR Sagittarius SD Scorpio	2015	Jan 20 to Feb 10 May 18 to Jun 10 Sep 16 to Oct 8	SR Aquarius SR Gemini SR Libra
2006	Mar 2 to Mar 24 July 4 to July 28 Oct 27 to Nov 17	SR Pisces SR Leo SD Cancer SR Scorpio	2016	Jan 4 to Jan 25 Apr 27 to May 21 Aug 29 to Sep 21 Dec 18 to Jan7 2017	SR Aquarius SD Capricorn SR Taurus SR Virgo SR Capricorn SD Sagittarius
2007	Feb 13 to Mar 7 Jun 15 to July 9 Oct 11 to Nov 1	SR Pisces SD Aquarius SR Cancer SR Scorpio SD Libra	2017	Apr 9 to May 2 Aug 12 to Sep 4 Dec 2 to Dec 22	SR Taurus SD Aries SR Virgo SD Leo SR Sagittarius
2008	Jan 27 to Feb 18 May 25 to Jun 18 Sep 23 to Oct 14	SR Aquarius SR Gemini SR Libra	2018	Mar 22 to Apr 14 July 25 to Aug 18 Nov 16 to Dec 5	SR Aries SR Leo SR Sagittarius SD Scorpio
2009	Jan 10 to Jan 31 May 6 to May 30 Sep 6 to Sep 28 Dec 25 to Jan 14 2010	SR Aquarius SD Capricorn SR Gemini SD Taurus SR Libra SD Virgo SR Capricorn	2019	Mar 4 to Mar 27 July 7 to July 31 Oct 30 to Nov 19	SR Pisces SR Leo SD Cancer SR Scorpio

YEAR	DATE	SIGN	YEAR	DATE	SIGN
2020	Feb 16 to Mar 9	SR Pisces	2028	Jan 23 to Feb 13	SR Aquarius
		SD Aquarius		May 20 to Jun 13	SR Gemini
	Jun 16 to July 11	SR Cancer		Sep 18 to Oct 10	SR Libra
	Oct 13 to Nov 2	SR Scorpio	2029	Jan 6 to Jan 26	SR Aquarius
		SD Libra			SD Capricorn
2021	Jan 29 to Feb 20	SR Aquarius		May 1 to May 24	SR Taurus
	May 29 to Jun 21	SR Gemini		Sep 1 to Sep 24	SR Libra
	Sep 25 to Oct 17	SR Libra			SD Virgo
				Dec 21 to Jan 10 2030	SR Capricorn
2022	Jan 13 to Feb 2	SR Aquarius	2030	Apr 12 to May 5	SR Taurus
		SD Capricorn			SD Aries
	May 9 to Jun 1	SR Gemini		Aug 15 to Sep 7	SR Virgo
		SD Taurus		Dec 5 to Dec 24	SR Capricorn
	Sep 8 to Oct 1	SR Libra			SD Sagittarius
		SD Virgo	2031	Mar 25 to Apr 17	SR Aries
	Dec 28 to Jan 17 2023	SR Capricorn		July 28 to Aug 21	SR Leo
2023	Apr 20 to May 14	SR Taurus		Nov 18 to Dec 8	SR Sagittarius
	Aug 22 to Sep 14	SR Virgo			SD Scorpio
	Dec 12 to Dec 31	SR Sagittarius	2032	Mar 6 to Mar 29	SR Aries
2024	Mar 31 to Apr 24	SR Aries			SD Pisces
	Aug 4 to Aug 27	SR Virgo		July 9 to Aug 2	SR Leo
		SD Leo			SD Cancer
	Nov 25 to Dec 14	SR Sagittarius		Nov 1 to Nov 21	SR Sagittarius
2025	Mar 14 to Apr 6	SR Aries			SD Scorpio
		SD Pisces	2033	Feb 17 to Mar 12	SR Pisces
	July 17 to Aug 10	SR Leo		Jun 20 to July 14	SR Cancer
	Nov 8 to Nov 28	SR Sagittarius		Oct 15 to Nov 5	SR Scorpio
		SD Scorpio			SD Libra
2026	Feb 25 to Mar 19	SR Pisces	2034	Feb 1 to Feb 22	SR Aquarius
	Jun 28 to July 22	SR Cancer		Jun 1 to Jun 25	SR Gemini
	Oct 23 to Nov 12	SR Scorpio		Sep 29 to Oct 20	SR Libra
2027	Feb 8 to Mar 2	SR Pisces	2035	Jan 16 to Feb 6	SR Aquarius
		SD Aquarius			SD Capricorn
	Jun 9 to July 3	SR Cancer		May 12 to Jun 5	SR Gemini
		SD Gemini			SD Taurus
	Oct 6 to Oct 27	SR Scorpio		Sep 12 to Oct 4	SR Libra
		SD Libra			SD Virgo

INDEX

A

accidents, 5
Adams, Brooks, 109
adaptation sensation, 31
Adkins, Christopher, 110
Adler, Alfred, 94
Albert, Prine, consort of
    Victoria, 92
Alda, Alan, 106
Aldrin, Edwin "Buzz", 105
Alger, Horatio, 92
Allen, Irwin, 101
Allen, Morty, 102
Allison, Luther, 107
Ambler, Eric, 113
Anderson, Jack, 103
Anderson, John, 102
Anderson, Loni, 116
Anderson, Marian, 98
Andrews, Roy Chapman, 95
Antiscion point, 14
Arbuckle, Fatty, 96
Arness, James, 103
Arquette, Rosanna, 110
ascendant
    Aries, 75
    Taurus, 76
    Gemini, 77
    Cancer, 78
    Leo, 79
    Virgo, 80
    Libra, 81
    Scorpio, 82
    Sagittarius, 83

Capricorn, 84
Auquarius, 85
Pisces, 86
aspect, 57
Assagioli, Roberto, 96
Astor, John Jacob, 91
Aurobindo, Sri, 112

B

Bacall, Lauren, 103
Bacon, Sir Francis, 91
Baer, Max, 100
Baha, Abdul, 93
Baker, Ginger, 116
Baker, Joe Don, 115
Bankhead, Tallulah, 98
Barris, Chuck, 105
Barrymore, Ethel, 95
Barrymore, John, 95
Barrymore, Lionel, 95
Bart, Belle, 96
Bartholdi, Frederic, 92
Bassett, Angela, 110
Baxter, Warner, 97
Beardsley, Aubrey, 94
Beckett, Samuel, 99
Beerbohm, Max, 94
Beery, Wallace, 95
Belafonte, Harry, 114
Belli, Melvin, 99
Benedict XV, Pope, 93
Benes, Eduard, 112
Bennett, Tony, 104
Benton, Barbi, 116

Berle, Milton, 99
Bernhardt, Sara, 93
Bernstein, Leonard, 101
Berrigan, Phillip, 103
Bikel, Theodore, 103
Black, Clint, 110
Blake, Amanda, 115
Bledsoe, Tempestt, 117
Bogdanovich, Peter, 107
Bok, Edward, 94
Bolger, Ray, 98
Bonaduce, Danny, 117
Borg, Bjorn, 117
Borges, Jorge Luis, 97
Borglum, Gutzon, 94
Borgnine, Ernest, 101
Boyer, Charles, 97
Bream, Julian, 115
Brennan, Walter, 97
Breyer, Steven, 115
Bronson, Charles, 102
Brooke, Rupert, 96
Brooks, Albert, 109
Brooks, Garth, 110
Brown, Edmund, Sr., 99
Brown, Helen Gurley, 102
Browning, Robert, 91
Brummel, George Bryan (Beau), 91
Bryant, Anita, 107
Brynner, Yul, 114
Buckley, Betty, 109
Burbank, Luther, 93
Burghoff, Gary, 108
Burnham, Daniel, 93
Burr, Raymond, 101
Burroughs, Edgar Rice, 97
Burstyn, Ellen, 105
Burton, Sir Richard, 92
Bushmiller, Ernie, 99

Byrd, Richard, 96
Byrnes, Ed "Kookie", 105

C
Caan, James, 107
Cabell, James Branch, 95
Caine, Michael, 115
Campbell, Glen, 107
Capaldi, Jim, 116
Capp, Al, 113
Cardinale, Claudia, 115
Carey, George, 93
Carlin, George, 106
Carlisle, Belinda, 110
Carnes, Kim, 116
Carpenter, Scott, 114
Carver, George Washington, 94
Cass, Peggy, 114
Cernan, Eugene, 106
Cervantes, 91
Chaffee, Roger, 106
Champion, Gower, 114
Chancellor, John, 104
Channing, Carol, 103
Charisse, Cyd, 102
Charles, Ray, 105
Child, Julia, 100
children, 31
Chopin, Frederic, 91
Christiansen, W. A., 95
Ciccone, Madonna, 110
Clayburgh, Jill, 109
Cliburn, Van, 106
Cobb, Irwin, 95
Cole, Natalie, 109
Coleman, Gary, 111
Collective Unconscious, 10
Colter, Jessi, 108
communication process, 35

Comte, Auguste, 91
contemplation, 9
Cooder, Ry, 109
Cooper, Leroy Gordon, 104
Copeland, Aaron, 98
Coppola, Francis Ford, 107
copying others, 29
Corot, Jean-Baptiste, 91
Cosell, Howard, 102
Coward, Noel, 97, 112
Cray, Robert, 110
Cromwell, Richard, 91
Crosby, Bing, 113
Crothers, Scatman, 100
Crystal, Billy, 109
Cummings, Constance, 113

D
Dali, Salvador, 98
Dana, Richard Henry, 92
Darin, Bobby, 115
Darrin, James, 106
Davis, Sammy, Jr., 104
Day, Dennis, 101
de Broglie, Prince Louis, 96
Decan, 13
DeCarlo, Yvonne, 103
defeatism, 15
Delaurentis, Dino, 101
Delibes, Leo, 92
Deluise, Dom, 105
Dempsey, Jack, 97
Denver, John, 116
Derek, John, 104
Dern, Bruce, 106
deVore, Nicholas, xv
Dewohl, Louis, 113
Dietrich, Marlene, 98
Dillon, Kevin, 111
Dinesen, Isak, 112

Dix, Dorothy, 94
Domino, Fats, 104
Donaldson, Sam, 106
Doré, Gustave Paul, 92
Dostoevsky, Feodor, 92
Douglas, Stephen A., 92
Dulles, John Foster, 96
Dumas, Alexandre, 91
Dunne, Griffin, 110
Durocher, Leo, 113

E
Earp, Wyatt, 93
Eastwood, Clint, 105
Ebert, Roger, 108
Eddy, Duane, 107
Edelfelt, Albert, 93
educational development, 30
Edward VII, 93
Edwards, Vince, 104
ego structure, 28
Elgar, Sir Edward, 94
Elizabeth (Consort of George VI), 98
Engels, Fredrich, 92
English, Richard, 100

F
Fabares, Shelly, 116
Falwell, Jerry, 115
Faulkner, William, 97
Feldon, Barbara, 116
Fernandez, Mary Joe, 111
Fielding, Henry, 91
Fitzgerald, Barry, 96
Fitzgerald, Ella, 101
Fitzgerald, F. Scott, 112
Flammarion, Camille, 93
Flynn, Errol, 100
Ford, Henry, II, 114

Forster, E. M., 95
Forte, Fabian, 116
Fowles, John, 104
Frakes, Johnathan, 110
Franciosa, Tony, 104
Franco, Francesco, 97
Frazier, Joe, 108
Freberg, Stan, 104
Friml, Rudolf, 95
Fromm, Erich, 98
Frost, David, 107
Fuller, Buckminister, 112

G
Gagarin, Yuri, 106
Galbraith, John Kenneth, 113
Galsworthy, John, 112
Gardner, Erle, Stanley, 96
Garfunkel, Art, 116
Garland, Judy, 103
Gauquelin, Francoise, 115
Gelbart, Larry, 104
George, Boy, 117
George, Henry, 92
George, Llewellyn, xi
Getty, Jean Paul, 97
Ghostley, Alice, 104
Gilbert, Melissa, 110
Gilford, Jack, 99
Giraudoux, Jean, 95
Gish, Lillian, 97
Glenn, John, 114
goal, 33
Golding, William, 113
Goldman, Emma, 94
Gordon, Richard, 105
Gorky, Maxim, 94
Gorman, Steve, 110
Gortner, Morjoe, 108
Gossett, Lou, Jr., 106

Gould, Chester, 98
Gould, Elliott, 107
Goulet, Robert, 106
Gowdy, Curt, 114
Grant, Cary, 98
Grayson, Kathryn, 114
Graziano, Rocky, 103
Greco, Buddy, 104
Greco, Jose, 101
Green, Lorne, 114
Grey, Joel, 105
Grimes, Tammy, 106
Grisham, John, 110
Grissom, Virgil "Gus," 104
Guthrie, Arlo, 109
Guttenberg, Steve, 110

H
Hackett, Buddy, 103
Hackman, Gene, 105
Haggard, H. Rider, 93
Hall, Manly Palmer, 98
Hall, Tom T., 106
Hamilton, George, 107
Hammerstein, Oscar, 112
Harrison, Rex, 99
Hart, William S., 112
Harte, Brett, 93
Harvey, Len, 113
Hauptmann, Bruno, 97, 113
Hayakawa, Sessue, 96
health, 23
Hearst, Patty, 117
Hefner, Hugh, 104
Hendryx, Nona, 109
Henie, Sonja, 100
Henner, Marilow, 109
Hitchcock, Alfred, 97
Hitler, Adolf, 37
Hogan, Ben, 100

Holden, William, 101
Hope, Bob, 98
Hopkins, Bo, 108
Hopper, Hedda, 96
Howard, Trevor, 101
Howe, James Wong, 97
Hoyle, Fred, 100
Hubbard, Elbert, 93
Hughes, Howard, 99, 113
Humbard, Rex, 101
Hunnicutt, Gayle, 116
Huston, John, 99
Hutton, Betty, 102
Huxley, Aldous, 97
Huxley, Thomas, 92

I
Ibsen, Henrik, 92
information gathering, 17
Ives, Burl, 100

J
Jackson, Victoria, 110
Joffre, Joseph, 93
Johnson, Ervin "Magic", 117
Jones, James Earl, 115
Janes, Quincy, 115
Jonson, Ben, 91
Joplin, Janis, 108

K
Karloff, Boris, 96
Keaton, Buster, 97
Keel, Howard, 101
Kelly, Gene, 100
Kelsey, Linda, 109
Kennedy, John F., 114
Kent, Rockwell, 95
Ketchum, Hank, 102
Key, Ted, 100

Keyserling, Hermann, 112
Kilmer, Joyce, 95
King, Albert, 103
King, Carole, 108
Kipling, Rudyard, 94
Kissinger, Henry, 103
Klee, Paul, 95
Klemperer, Werner, 102
Koestler, Arthur, 99
Kopechne, Mary Jo, 108

L
Laine, Frankie, 100
Lamarr, Hedy, 100
Lanchester, Elsa, 98
Lane, Abbie, 115
Laurie, Arthur, 94
Lawrence, D. H., 112
Lear, William, 98
Learned, Michael, 107
Lee, Michelle, 116
Lee, Ruta, 106
Leek, Sybil, 103
Leigh, Janet, 115
Lemon, Meadowlark, 115
Lendl, Ivan, 110
Lenier, Jules, 105
Leo, Alan, 94
Leonard, Sugar Ray, 110
Le Petomane (Joseph Pujol), 93
Lewis, Anthony, 114
Lewis, Meriwether, 91
Lilly, William, 91
Lester, Joseph, 92
Lodge, Henry Cabot, II, 98
Lollabrigida, Gina, 104
Lombardo, Guy, 98
Lopez, Trini, 107
Lord, Jack, 105
Louis XVI, 91

Lowell, Percival, 93
Luboff, Norman, 101
Lucas, George, 116
Lugosi, Bela, 95
Lumiere, Auguste, 94
Lunar Return, 25
Lynley, Carol, 108
Lytton, Lady (Wife of Bulwer-Lytton), 91

M
MacNamara, Robert, 101
MacNee, Patrick, 102
MacRae, Gordon, 102
Mailer, Norman, 103
Malden, Karl, 100
Malraux, Andre, 98
Mandrall, Louise, 110
Marciano, Rocky, 103
Markham, Edwin, 93
Marsalis, Wynton, 110
Marsh, Jean, 106
Marsh, Ngaio, 97
Marshell, Thurgood, 99
Martin, Mary, 113
Martin, Steve, 109
Marx, Harpo, 97
Matlin, Marlee, 117
Mature, Victor, 101
Mauldin, Bill, 102
Mayall, John, 115
Maybank, Thomas, 94
Mayfield, Curtis, 108
Moynihan, Daniel Patrick, 104
Mays, Willie, 105
McCartney, Paul, 108
McCormack, John, 96
McCormick, Pat, 106
McDivitt, James, 105
McDonald, Pat, 109

McGraw, Ali, 107
McKern, Leo, 102
McKuen, Rod, 107
McPherson, Aimee Semple, 96
McWhirter, Ross, 114
meditation, 9
    Aries, 76
    Taurus, 77
    Gemini, 78
    Cancer, 79
    Leo, 80
    Virgo, 81
    Libra, 82
    Scorpio, 83
    Sagittarius, 84
    Capricorn, 85
    Aquarius, 86
    Pisces, 87
Menuhin, Yehudi, 101
Mercury retrograde, 1, 14
    anecdotes, 19
    behind the veil of, 4
    the downside, 15
    events, 121–185
    famous people, 89
    in the houses, 57
    manifests, 13
    periods, 22, 75
    positions 1900–2035, 187
    progressed, 14
    projects, 16
    in the signs, 41
    the upside, 16
Mercury retrograde in houses
    1st House, 58
    2nd House, 60
    3rd House, 61
    4th House, 62
    5th House, 63
    6th House, 64

7th House, 65
8th House, 67
9th House, 68
10th House, 69
11th House, 71
12th House, 72
Mercury retrograde in signs
    in Aries, 42
    in Taurus, 43
    in Gemini, 44
    in Cancer, 45
    in Leo, 46
    in Virgo, 48
    in Libra, 49
    in Scorpio, 50
    in Sagittarius, 51
    in Capricorn, 52
    in Aquarius, 53
    in Pisces, 54
Mesmer, F. A., 91
messages, 5
metaphysics of the process, 8
Meyer, Cord, Jr., 102
Mifune, Toshire, 114
Miller, Arthur, 100
Miller, Henry, 96
Milligan, Spike, 114
Mills, John, 99
Moffo, Anna, 115
Mollison, James, 99
money, 18
Montalban, Ricardo, 114
Montgomery, Little Brother, 113
Montgomery, Robert, 99
Moon, 5
Morehead, Agnes, 99
Morganstern, Christian, 94
Morris, William, 92
Mostel, Zero, 100

Muldaur, Diana, 107
Muni, Paul, 97
Munro, Roy de L., 96
Murphy, George, 98
Musial, Stan, 102

N
Nabokov, Vladimir, 97
Nadar, Ralph, 106
Namath, Joe, 108
Nash, Graham, 108
negative thinking, 15
Nelson, Ozzie, 99
Nielsen, Leslie, 103
Norton, Ken, 109
Nostradamus, Michel, 91
Nourrit, Jacqueline, 114
Novello, Antonia, 116
Nuthall, Betty, 110
Nuyen, France, 107

O
Oakley, Annie, 94
O'Brien, Margaret, 106
occurences, famous, 119
O'Connor, Donald, 104
Odetta, 105
O'Hair, Madelyn Murray, 101
opportunities, karmic, 24
O'Sullivan, Maureen, 113
O'Toole, Peter, 115

P
Paar, Jack, 101
Paderewski, Ignace, 112
Page, Patti, 104
Papp, Joseph, 114
Parker, Bonnie, 100
Parker, Eleanor, 103
Parker, Fess, 104

Pasternak, Boris, 112
Patchen, Kenneth, 113
Patti, Adelina, 93
Paul VI, Pope, 97
Pauling, Linus, 113
Pavarotti, Liuciano, 106
Perkins, Anthony, 105
Perkins, Carl, 105
Peron, Juan, 97
pessimism, 15
Peters, Bernadette, 109
Phillip, Prince (Consort of
    Queen Elizabeth II), 102
Piccard, Jean and Auguste, 95
Pickford, Mary, 112
Pitman, Sir Isaac, 92
Pius XI, Pope, 94
Planetary Return, 26
Plimpton, George, 104
Poder, Portia, 101
Powell, John Wesley, 92
Preminger, Otto, 99
problems, automobile, 5
psychological patterns, 27
Pulitizer, Joseph, 93

R
Ramakrishna, 92
Ranier, Prince of Monaco, 103
Ravel, Maurice, 95
Reagan, Nancy, 102
Reddy, Helen, 108
reflection, 9, 17
Regardie, Francis Israel, 99
Reinhardt, Django, 100
Renan, Ernest, 92
retrograde cannot "cause"
    anything, 5
review, 17
Reynolds, Burt, 115

Reynolds, Debbie, 105
Reynolds, Sir Joshua, 91
Rickenbacker, Eddie, 112
Ringwald, Molly, 111
Rivera, Diego, 95
Roberts, Pernell, 105
Robinson, Brooks, 107, 116
Robson, Vivian, 96
Rockefeller, David, 114
Rockefeller, Nelson, 99
Rockne, Knute, 96
Rodgers, Jimmie, 112
Rodgers, Richard, 98
Rogers, Kenny, 115
Rogers, Wayne, 115
Ross, Katharine, 108
Roth, Phillip, 105
Rundgren, Todd, 109
running in circles, 33
Rusk, Dean, 100
Russell, George (A. E.), 112
Russell, Mark, 105
Russell, Rosalind, 100

S
Sadat, Anwar, 101
Sagan, Francoise, 106
St. James, Susan, 116
Ste. Marie, Buffy, 108
Salk, Jonas, 113
Sampras, Pete, 117
Sandburg, Carl, 95
Schmidt, Helmut, 101
Schulman, Martin, 2
Schumann, Robert, 91
Schwab, Charles, 94
Scott, Randolph, 113
Scriabin, Alexander, 94
Sedgwick, Kyra, 111
Sennett, Mack, 95

Serling, Rod, 103
Severinsen, Doc, 104
Sharif, Omar, 105
Shaw, Artie, 100
Shearer, Norma, 113
Shearing, George, 102
Sheedy, Ally, 110
Sheen, Martin, 116
Shelley, Carole, 107
Silverman, Jonathan, 117
Simon, Neil, 115
Simon, Paul, 116
Simpson, O. J., 109
Sinclair, Upton, 112
skills
    communication, 39
    productive, 36
Smuts, Jan Christian, 94
Solar Return, 25
Solzhenitzyn, Aleksandr, 101
Sousa, John Phillip, 112
Spaak, Catherine, 115
Springfield, Dusty, 116
Stalin, Joseph, 112
Stamp, Terrance, 108
Stanwyck, Barbara, 99
Stapleton, Jean, 114
Starr, Ringo, 116
Stauback, Roger, 108
Steiger, Rod, 103
Steinbeck, John, 98
Stern, Isaac, 102
Stevens, Andrew, 110
Stevens, Cat, 109
Stout, Rex, 96
Stowe, Madeleine, 110
Stravinsky, Igor, 95
Strummer, Joe, 117
Sun, 5
    in Aries, 75
    in Taurus, 76
    in Gemini, 77
    in Cancer, 78
    in Leo, 79
    in Virgo, 80
    in Libra, 81
    in Scorpio, 82
    in Sagittarius, 83
    in Capricorn, 84
    in Aquarius, 85
    in Pisces, 86
Sutherland, Donald, 106
Sutter, John, 91
Swayze, John Cameron, 99

T
Taylor, Rod, 115
Tenno, Yoshihito Taisho, 95
Thomas, Clarence, 109
Thomas, Dylan, 113
Thomas, Helen, 102
Thomas, Michael Tilson, 108
thought-form, 33
Tillis, Mel, 105
Tierney, Gene, 102
Todd, Thelma, 113
Tolkien, J. R. R., 96
Torre, Joe, 107
Toscanini, Arturo, 94
Tracy, Spencer, 98
transit, 14
Travanti, Daniel, 107
traveling, 17
Travolta, John, 117
Treacher, Arthur, 97
Trebec, Alex, 108
Trevino, Lee, 107
Trikonis, Gus, 107
Truman, Harry, 95
Twiggy, 116

U
Udall, Mo, 103
Uggams, Leslie, 108
unconscious factors, 23

V
Valli, Frankie, 107
Van Dyke, Dick, 104
Van Gogh, Vincent, 111
Van Patten, Joyce, 106
Van Peebles, Melvin, 105
Veljohnson, Reginald, 109
Vigoda, Abe, 102
Villa, Pancho, 112
Von Richthofen, Manfred,
    112

W
Wallace, George, 114
Wallace, Mike, 114
Waller, Fats, 99
Warren, Robert Penn, 99

Webb, Jack, 114
West, Mae, 96
Wilander, Mats, 110, 117
Wilde, Oscar, 93
Wilkins, Sir George, 96
Williams, Clarence III, 116
Williams, Hank, 103
Williams, Hank, Jr., 109
Williams, Mason, 107
Williams, Ted, 101
Wilson, Brian, 108
Wonder, Stevie, 109
Woodhull, Victoria, 92
Wyler, William, 98

Y
Yarborough, Cale, 107
Yastrzemski, Carl, 116
Yorty, Sam, 100

Z
Zola, Emile, 93

Sandy Gibson

Robert Wilkinson is a practicing professional astrologer with more than 25 years experience as a counselor, lecturer, author, and cultural philosopher. Robert graduated from the University of Texas at Austin in 1972 with a BA in psychology specializing in social psychology and historical cycles. His post graduate work included personal and group counseling techniques, and extended studies in Eastern philosophies and the Ageless Wisdom. He has an active national and international practice, and is in demand as a speaker across North America.

Robert invites you to send in your most unusual, outrageous, or improbable Mercury retrograde experience. If enough people respond, he thinks an interesting book could be assembled from the anecdotes. The ephemeris in the back of the book can be of help to determine if Mercury was retrograde during the event. He looks forward to hearing from readers! Write him at Box 24A09, Los Angeles, CA 90024-1009.